PS- 11(61-62) 333

MAN AND MORALS

D. J. B. HAWKINS

MAN
AND MORALS

SHEED AND WARD
LONDON AND NEW YORK

FIRST PUBLISHED 1960
SHEED AND WARD LTD.
33 MAIDEN LANE
LONDON W.C.2
AND
SHEED AND WARD INC.
64 UNIVERSITY PLACE
NEW YORK 3

IMPRIMATUR
DATUM SOUTHWARCI DIE IA MARTII 1960
H. GIBNEY V.G.

NIHIL OBSTAT
D. FOGARTY, D.D., L.C.L.
CENSOR DEPUTATUS

THIS BOOK IS SET IN 11 on 12-PT. BEMBO BY
FLETCHER AND SON LTD NORWICH AND BOUND BY
THE LEIGHTON-STRAKER BOOKBINDING CO. LTD, LONDON

CONTENTS

v

CONTENTS

FOREWORD

SYSTEMATIC philosophy has become less and less fashionable in this country in recent years. This, however, is an old-fashioned survey of the field of ethics. It does not make its start from any special oddity of the logic or language of morals but, after two introductory chapters on the nature of man, tries to offer a first degree of intelligibility for the whole field, in the light of which more detailed studies can be undertaken with greater confidence. It is to be hoped that some minds still work most easily in this way.

I am convinced that morality leads naturally to religion, and have tried to suggest how it does so in the brief concluding chapter. But I think that it is altogether unfair to the secular moralist to treat ethics from the beginning as if it made no sense without religious considerations. Hence I have conducted the discussion on the purely human level, leaving it to be understood that as a theist I should want to add what is said about "God the Lawgiver" in Chapter IX of my *Essentials of Theism* but need not be repeated here.

Chapter IV, on "Free Will and Right Action", is based on an article which appeared under the same title in the *Modern Schoolman* (St. Louis) for May 1949. It needed extensive rewriting, but I am grateful for permission to reprint what survived this process, as also to the Columbia University Press for permission to reproduce the long quotation from Dr. Albert G. A. Balz's *Cartesian Studies* at the beginning of Chapter II.

D. J. B. H.

Chapter I

MAN AS A THINKING BEING

I

THERE is a traditional discrimination between, on the one hand, sensation and mental activity on the sensory level and, on the other, thought and mental activity on the intellectual level. We have to ask whether such a clearcut distinction can be made and, if so, where precisely it occurs.

In modern times two influences have tended towards the denial of any clearcut distinction between sensation and thought. They have come to be regarded as differing not in kind but in complexity. The empirical movement in philosophy has set out to interpret all levels of mental activity in terms of the inter-relatedness of sensations and images without the intervention of any higher energy. Evolutionary theories of cosmic history tend to iron out differences of kind with the aid of series of inter-mediary types which exhibit only a gradual and continuous development.

On reflection the argument from evolution does not seem to be a very strong one. Unless the history of the universe consists simply in having more and more (or less and less) of what has always been, new kinds of factor must emerge from time to time. If, for example, there was a period when nothing possessed sensation, the first sensitive organism, of however rudimentary a sort it may have been, marked the emergence of a wholly new kind of factor in reality. There is no reason in principle why thinking should not be an equally new emergent factor. It is, of course, precisely the merit of Hegel's philosophical analysis of evolution that it recognizes the necessity by which quantitative change gives rise to change of quality. The adequacy of mere gradualness is an imaginative impression which does not survive critical reflection.

If, however, Hume and his followers have succeeded in explaining all human mental activity in terms of sensations and images, there is no need to introduce any other factor. Thinking will then simply be a name for some of the more complicated forms of an activity which is essentially of the same kind. But we should first examine how the distinction between sensation and thought has been traditionally understood. It may be that it needs amendment rather than abolition.

II

The traditional basis of distinction which first comes to mind is, no doubt, that sensation is awareness of particulars and thought is awareness of universals. That is what we find in Aristotle, but for its origins we must look behind Aristotle to Plato. We should beware, however, of supposing that Plato was concerned with exactly the same sort of problem.

The burden of the *Theaetetus*, for example, is that knowledge is not to be identified with perception but involves a kind of judgment which goes beyond mere perception. What we might be tempted to call judgments of perception, registrations of the pure empirical datum, belong in this division entirely to the side of perception. Judgment, for Plato, does not begin until standards are applied to the empirical datum. The *Theaetetus* does not make clear what precisely these standards should be. Plato is evidently feeling his way towards something more satisfying than the Socratic doctrine of forms, but he has not yet arrived. The *Theaetetus* leaves us with a sharp distinction between mere experience and the application of standards of judgment to experience, but it does not succeed in defining what the appropriate standards of judgment are.

The relative obscurity of this question in *Plato's* mature philosophy is perhaps the reason why more attention has been paid to the problem as formulated in terms of the Socratic doctrine of forms. The classical passage here is, of course, the Divided Line at the end of the sixth book of the *Republic*. For our present purposes it will be sufficient to say that Plato distinguishes between mere appearance or mere experience, which seem to be equated, and an awareness of the forms, first as participated by empirical objects, then in themselves, and finally in their systematic unity and relationship to the Good. Knowledge does not begin before the first dim glimpse of the forms.

The distinctions which Plato makes are not between animal and human awareness; they are between stages of human mentality. Nor are these distinctions between a perception of singulars and a knowledge of universals; the first stage of genuine knowledge is concerned with singulars, but knowledge does not begin in the proper sense until singulars are judged in their relation to standards or ideals, whether we think of these as universal or not.

Our common presuppositions are the result of what Aristotle did to Plato's thinking, and we should note that the material for Aristotle's critical reflection is to be found less in Plato's more mature but less clearcut speculations than in the original Socratic doctrine of forms. Aristotle thought that he had seen more clearly than the later Plato the nature of the mistake which made the doctrine of forms liable to so many objections. What had to be done was to make the forms into constituents of singulars. Instead of ideal standards they would be universal essences. The distinctively human stage of mentality lay in the power to abstract and to contemplate universal essences.

Hence the systematic psychology of the *De Anima* presents us with two levels of mentality. The lower level, which is common to men and to animals, is an awareness of singulars through the senses. But Aristotle realized better than most of his commentators the subjective character of sensation by itself. In order

3

that there should be perception of external objects something more was required. The function of external perception was attributed to the sensibility as a whole, the common sense, which had the power of apprehending quantity and its modes, the common sensibles. The central sensibility had also certain other functions which Aristotle regarded as belonging to the working of mind on the sense-level, such as imagination and memory and instincts of choice and avoidance.

The intellect was, then, both a power of abstraction and a power of contemplating the universal essences thus abstracted. Hence it was both active and passive, and Aristotle emphasized the difference between the individual passive intellect and an apparently impersonal active intellect in an odd way which need not bother us here. Having formed abstract concepts, the intellect is able to apply them to real subjects or to assert their mutual relations in the act of judgment and to combine judgments in trains of reasoning. This intellectual level of mentality is peculiar to man.

Such is the familiar Aristotelian account of the two levels of mind. It may be observed at once that it lets us in for some of the more embarrassing problems of the Aristotelian tradition. It commits us to a doctrine of clearcut specific essences which raises difficulties in an evolving universe. It makes us ask how these essences are individuated, as if individuality were not a primary and self-explanatory character of the real. And it makes us wonder how we have an intellectual knowledge of the individual at all. These problems would have to be faced if reflection on experience showed that the Aristotelian account was adequate and needed no modification. But this critical reflection on experience has to be made.

III

The classical empiricists, Locke, Berkeley and Hume, are often thought to have refuted the traditional doctrine of universals.

What they more precisely did was to refute what may be called the sausage-machine theory of thought. Prone as we are to materialize our ideas, we may come to think of abstraction on the analogy of popping a sense-datum or phantasm into the active intellect at one end and waiting for a neat abstract concept to emerge at the other for the admiring contemplation of the passive intellect. Reflection on experience shows that there is no such thing as an abstract concept which is an object of awareness in the same way as a sense-datum or a material thing. Of course we think in universal terms; of course we apprehend similarities and classify things with regard to them. But this is a new way of being aware of objects; it is not the production of a new kind of object.

The fatal weakness of empiricism at this juncture, a weakness which becomes fully explicit in Hume, was to suppose that, in correcting a misleading analogy about the nature of thought, the distinction between sensation and thought had been abolished. We must, however, acknowledge another success for empiricist method. Hume succeeded in presenting a plausible picture of a kind of mental life in terms simply of sensations and images. A great deal of behaviour which we should be inclined to regard as dependent on an *awareness* of the situation could be interpreted with reference only to the *occurrence* of sensations and images. This sort of behaviourism has been renewed in our own time with similar plausibility by Professor Ryle.

Yet the fact of awareness is an immediate datum of human consciousness. We are aware that we are aware, and that awareness is an activity irreducible to anything else. Grammatically it would be permissible to go on to say that we are aware that we are aware that we are aware, and so on, but this is not a complexity which enters into the real situation. In the real situation awareness of the primary object and awareness of awareness are a unity. Awareness is of its nature reflective. Analytic thinking and the observation of similarities on the one hand, and synthetic thinking, the apprehension of entailments and the consequent

5

possibility of reasoning, on the other, are modes of differentiation of an original and distinctive activity which we may continue to call simply awareness.

What is the upshot of this meditation? It would seem that the original and irreducible human factor is what we have called awareness. It may also be called the power of reflection or self-consciousness, but this is because awareness is essentially reflexive or self-conscious, not because reflection in its elementary form needs to supervene upon some more primary form of direct awareness. It belongs equally to awareness to be capable of various sorts of differentiation of attention, among which must be included the observation of similarities and the ability to think in universal terms. But thinking in universal terms is not the whole story about thought; it presupposes that simple awareness of fact which is the primary form of thought.

It remains that Hume's description of mind is a very ingenious account of how mind may work at the purely animal level. There is no reason to attribute to animals the power of awareness in the distinctive sense in which we have equated it with the fundamental energy of thought. Animal behaviour can be interpreted on the basis of the mere occurrence of sensations and images. If, then, we speak of an animal as "aware" of its environment, this is in a very different sense from what is meant by human awareness. It has to be interpreted behaviouristically, in so far as the occurrence of sensations and images enables an animal to react to its environment in a way which for a human being involves awareness as a distinctive activity.

Human awareness or thought is, therefore, an original emergent factor in the history of the world, inexplicable in terms of anything that went before it. The Aristotelian distinction of mind on the level of sense and mind on the level of intellect requires not abolition but amendment. Aristotle over-intellectualized sensation and failed to grasp the full nature of thinking. The dividing-line is to be drawn one stage earlier, at the appearance of awareness in its proper and distinctive meaning.

IV

This doctrine, which is obviously a simplification of prevalent notions, may indeed seem to be an oversimplification of what is commonly regarded as a complex problem. But surely it is not unnatural that there should be a fairly obvious reason why man alone of all the animals has sciences, arts, morals and religion. At any rate this is submitted as a solution of the problem which, apart from the special conditions under which European philosophy has developed and apart from our inveterate tendency to anthropomorphize animal behaviour, ought to commend itself easily to reflection.

By way of filling out the context, we may begin with the truisms that a thing must be in order to be aware and that to be aware is always to be aware of something. No doubt we can go on to construct fictitious objects, but this presupposes the awareness of the real objects which provide their material. Here lies the importance of sentience for human knowledge. For consciousness is primitively an awareness of our sensations; sensations are the stuff of our experience. It is an empirical fact that we are not conscious of our embodiedness except in so far as we have sensations, although in being aware of sensation we become aware also of some part of the extended organism as the background and bearer of sensation.

Yet awareness is not only consciousness of the self as affected by sensation; it includes also the perception of external objects. The power of awareness is precisely the way in which a thing can transcend itself and communicate with what is other than itself. If this belongs to the very nature of awareness, it is a mistake to suppose that all knowledge of things other than the self must be inferential. No doubt it does not occur apart from data of consciousness, but it does not follow that it must be inferred from such data. Everything points to the fact that our fundamental awareness of an external world is logically direct, whatever conditions it presupposes. If we were confined to

7

inference, we might conclude that there was some cause of our sensations, but it might be anything whatever, perhaps of an entirely unknown nature.

While, however, the majority of perceptual judgments are inferences from sensation of greater or less probability, they seem to presuppose some basic intuitive knowledge that an external material world exists. This would appear to reside in the experience of contact, not through any special privilege of tactile sensation but because in contact there is mutual compression of mass. There we have not merely a causal transaction but an assimilation, the communication of and sharing in an identical sort of corporeal modification. In this case we are intuitively aware of another body with which we are in contact. With this we may compare the experience of intuitive memory, when some event in the past genuinely reproduces itself in our consciousness instead of our having in the usual way to try to recapture the past by a hazardous effort of imagination. So also we have intuitive knowledge of other minds in moments of complete sympathy and communication, and there is the same contrast with our usual more or less reliable attempts to interpret other minds through the evidence of speech and gesture. Hence, while much more than we might suppose of our presumed knowledge of the external world, of our own past and of other minds, is inferential and remains within the sphere of greater or less probability, all these convictions have a basis of intuitive awareness without which the merely probable judgments would be enormously less probable.

It will be noticed that on this account perception and memory in the full sense of the words are held to be intellectual acts. What we might call "perception" and "memory" in the case of an animal are to be interpreted in terms of behaviour due to the mere occurrence of sensations and images. To make an application to the case in which we are most tempted to anthropomorphize, a dog's "recognition" of its master is not more than behaviour stimulated by a familiar and gratifying smell and sound. But analysis of the Humian sort has shown so clearly how much even of human behaviour might be interpreted with no further assumption that we should not regard its application to animals as paradoxical. It is only a pity that Hume's analysis of mind was not originally put forward as a contribution to animal psychology. For reflection informs men that they have a factor of explicit awareness or thought for which Hume made no room.

V

We might also fill out the context in another way by asking to what sort of general philosophy this conception of thought leads. We mentioned at the beginning that the insistence on the universal as the primary object of thought entailed some of the more embarrassing problems of the Aristotelian tradition. To hold that thought is primarily an awareness of real singular things enables us to escape these problems. But does it provide an opening for a metaphysic at all? We may remember that in the time of William of Ockham the doctrine of an intellectual intuition of the singular was accompanied by a gradual retreat from metaphysics. Are we perhaps entering on the same road?

If we answer that our account enables us to replace a metaphysic of essence by a metaphysic of existence, this has, of course, nothing whatever to do with what is nowadays called existentialism. We refer rather to an aspect of Aquinas's philosophy which has received a greater emphasis from Gilson and some other modern Thomists than it did from Aquinas himself. St. Thomas, in his philosophical theology, exploits a conception of being in which being is envisaged as the fundamental energy of things and things are differentiated by the various limits within which they exhibit being. The world is seen not as a collection of essences which happen to be instantiated but as the field in which being assumes its multitudinous forms. This, if it is

9

accepted, becomes the obligatory opening of the systematic metaphysic which St. Thomas never wrote.

But this is also precisely how our account of thinking would lead us to approach metaphysics. For us the first deliverance of thought is the existential judgment. Something exists. Every such something has an individual quiddity which being assumes and under which being is manifested. We can go on to observe the multifarious resemblances and differences of things without being tied down to any more rigid apparatus of fixed types than we actually turn out to find in experience. We can notice the clusters of resemblance in which specific types consist without having to regard the type as a prior unity which has to be somehow individualized.

This is surely the way to a genuine metaphysic of being. We may regret that the fourteenth-century philosophers, in over-throwing Scotus's metaphysic of essence, could not conceive an alternative and better metaphysic and turned away from meta-physics altogether. There is no need to make the same mistake again. It should now be possible on a really empirical foundation —that is to say, on our intellectual experience of individual existence—to develop the metaphysic of being which was adumbrated by Aquinas in the thirteenth century.

VI

Sensations are in themselves pleasant or painful in so far as the sentient organism instinctively feels them as ministering to or indicating either its fulfilment or its frustration. It is not merely the awareness of sensation which is pleasant or painful. No doubt it is pleasant to be aware of our own pleasant sensations, and painful to be aware of our own painful sensations. Awareness of the sensations of others, however, may be accompanied by complete indifference, by the pleasures and pains of sympathy, or even by the painful grudging of their pleasure and a sadistic pleasure in their pain. Pleasure and pain, then, occur first of all at the purely sensory level, below the level of awareness proper, and they lead at that level to behaviour directed towards the continuance and enhancement of pleasure and the avoidance of pain.

Awareness of sensation as pleasant or painful is at the same time awareness of the conative aspect of sense-experience, of our tendencies towards pleasure and away from pain. With the full development of thought the conative aspect of experience becomes more complex. Instead of the mere immediately pleasant and immediately painful we become aware of other aspects under which things call for pursuit or avoidance. We call them in different ways good or evil, and the same thing may be under one respect good or deserving of pursuit and under another evil or deserving of avoidance. But all this development is rooted in the distinction between the fulfilment or frustration, immediate or eventual, of our nature or of another's, of which the most elementary manifestation is the felt contrast of sensory pleasure and pain.

When we are confronted with different possibilities which are good in different ways, we have to choose between them. No doubt a comparison often leaves only one possible choice with any attraction for us, so that we necessarily choose it. But we shall try to show that there are cases when we are left with a final freedom of choice. For such choices we are ultimately responsible, and, since what is good in one respect may be evil in another, we are responsible for the evil in what we choose as well as for the good. If we say that what seems good to us may not be morally good, we must also try to explain what is meant by moral good and evil. The point at the moment is simply that a thinking being is also necessarily a moral being.

Chapter II

SOUL AND BODY

I

To some minds St. Thomas Aquinas's doctrine of man as having an immortal soul which is yet, in the Aristotelian sense, the form of the bodily organism, appears to be a perhaps heroic but ultimately ineffectual attempt to combine the advantages of two inconsistent points of view. In the end, it may seem, we must choose between thoroughgoing materialism and the Platonic and Cartesian view that the soul is essentially an independent entity although it inhabits and uses the body for a time. Here is the way in which one critic puts it.

Under what conditions can Thomistic man escape identification with organismic or naturalistic man? How can we follow the good counsel never to lose sight of the fact that it is the man who feels and thinks and, nevertheless, avoid the conclusion that all the historic distinctions summed up in the distinction between body and soul are nothing more than a distinction between organization and that which, in relation to the purposes of an inquiry, may be regarded as the raw materials of the organization? In great perplexity, I can but suggest this answer: Thomistic man is not organismic man, because the former is astonishingly like Cartesian man ... How can all the conditions be fulfilled unless St. Thomas admits, as an abiding truth, *that man is a soul using a body?* I must confess my inability to see how Thomistic man can meet all the conditions for which it was devised, escape reduction to the organismic or naturalistic pattern, and provide a program for scientific inquiries, unless that program be based upon a radically "dualistic" conception of man's constitution.[1]

Yet it is difficult to avoid the impression that the Platonic and Cartesian tradition arrives too easily at the assertion of human immortality. If the soul were so clearly an independent entity, it would seem that we ought to have some much more positive conception of the life of a disembodied soul and, indeed, that our present experience should not be as thoroughly subject to bodily conditions as it is. In reality our whole normal experience is of an embodied self, and we have only the vaguest conception of what a disembodied experience might be. The average man's idea of life after death is still obviously dependent on the primitive notion of a ghost, a body which is yet somehow not a body, but a consistent view of life after death is hard to attain.

Nevertheless there is also at first sight something about man to which mere materialism is evidently inadequate. Since man is unique in being able to think of death and of an afterwards, it would be odd if a being capable of thinking *sub specie aeternitatis* were to be so ingloriously extinguished after so short a time. However essentially man may be a material being, the burden of proof is on those who wish to hold that he is nothing else. Whether a hylomorphic doctrine of man is able to provide an acceptable middle course is worth exploring. But we must first say something about the Aristotelian theory of matter and form in general.

II

The elementary analogy to which Aristotle's various uses of the categories of matter and form refer is evident enough in his own example of the carving of a statue. Here form is quite literally

[1] Albert G. A. Balz, *Cartesian Studies*, New York, 1951, pp. 308-10.

13

shape. The sculptor's art gives the block of marble a new and significant shape. In terms of substance we should, at least now-adays, interpret this as a relatively permanent pattern or system of relations involving a vast number of units of substance when the rest are hewn away. It is not difficult, however, to employ the analogy, as Aristotle does, in respect of the actual attributes and activities belonging to a substance at any one time. These are, so to say, the actual shape which its substantial potentialities assume in these or those actual circumstances. We can appro-priately, in Aristotelian language, call them its accidental forms.

The application of the categories of matter and form within the realm of substance itself results from considering substantial change, the case in which a thing does not merely pass into a different manifestation of the same substantial potentialities but becomes a different kind of thing with new potentialities. Take the difference between mixing wine with water and combining hydrogen and oxygen to make water. In the former instance there is no essential change; all that you have is a weak and watery wine in place of the true, the blushful Hippocrene. In the latter, water has a quite different appearance and effect from hydrogen and oxygen in isolation. That the elements of hydrogen and oxygen in fact persist and can be isolated once more by a reverse chemical change only sharpens the analogy, for it shows that the specific qualities of water belong to the structure, or rather to the hydrogen and oxygen as structured. A chemical molecule is a structure with specific powers which do not belong to its elements in isolation. To speak of such a structure as a substantial form is a natural application of the original analogy.

Aristotle himself extends the analogy to what he takes to be the ultimate corporeal particles and regards them as constituted by an entirely undifferentiated substratum, which is prime matter, and the first principles of determinate potentiality, which are the primary substantial forms. This was an easy inference to make in terms of the science of his day. If the four elements of fire, air, water and earth, which each manifested its characteristic pair of the elementary qualities of hot and cold, dry and wet, were capable of transmutation one into the other, the substratum of change must be something which neither existed by itself nor possessed any observable quality.

This line of argument is no longer open to us. The modern physicist, while pursuing his analysis as far as possible, does not dogmatize about what the ultimate elements of the corporeal world may turn out to be, nor, consequently, does he assert that they must be capable of transmutation one into another. Nevertheless the philosopher may still ask for a metaphysical analysis of what it means to be corporeal. A bodily thing is a mass of determinate volume with a determinate type of activity. In even the simplest body there is the antithesis of determinacy of form and character and the indeterminacy of mere voluminousness. For voluminousness in general, as apart from being this specific shape and size, is a character of pure indeterminacy, of the dissipation of being. To this fundamental peculiarity of the spatial mode of being we may still refer under the name of first matter, which thus holds its place in a metaphysical analysis of what it is to be corporeal. It is, indeed, only such a metaphysical conception of first matter which would justify Aristotle's assertion that matter in itself not only has no observable quality but is absolutely devoid of any actual predicate in any category whatsoever.[1]

Returning to the direction of greater complexity, we may note that a living organism, as self-maintaining, self-developing and self-reproducing, is, like a chemical combination but in a more striking way, a structure whose powers exceed those of its constituents taken in isolation. The character of an organism does not need to be explained by a vital principle or entelechy which is a distinct thing, a kind of managing director governing the activity of the whole. This is mythology, but the Aristotelian

---

[1] Cf. *Metaphysics*, Z 3, 1029 a 20-21. In contrast the argument in *De Generatione et Corruptione*, I 3, could by itself be interpreted as leading to the physical hypothesis of a non-perceptible but not necessarily indeterminate substratum of the four elements.

conception of substantial form or structure is a precise description of the observed fact. Scientific investigation, of course, suggests that the substantial unit of life is the cell and that an organism should be considered as a natural pattern of cells rather than as a strict unity of substance and activity.

A strict unity of substance belongs to the organism which is sentient, for sentience is a field of experience pervading the organism as a whole. To describe the unity of sentience as a substantial form is, evidently, to give another turn to the meaning of this expression, for a field of experience is not simply a corporeal structure. Sensations are not in themselves voluminous; they do not occupy space. To that extent they are incorporeal. But reflection on our own sentient experience, which is the only means of investigation open to us, shows it as belonging to the organism. Our awareness of ourselves as embodied cannot in the concrete be separated from our consciousness of sensation. Bodily consciousness does not occur in the absence of specific sensation, and every specific sensation carries with it some degree of bodily consciousness. The bodily organism and the field of sense-experience are not, therefore, separate things. To describe the sentient psyche as a higher form of the organism and as composing a substantial unity with it is only to do justice to the unity of bodily and sentient consciousness.

Even when, in the case of man, we must take reflective awareness into account as well as sentience, it is clear that our normal thinking presupposes sentience. The evidence for special instances of cognition independent of sentience is not to be despised, but such cognition is plainly abnormal. Many of us could not assert that we have ever had any such experience, and even those who would claim to have had it have only to be asked what their experience would amount to if it were restricted to such instances for it to be seen that they are at least altogether exceptional.

Thinking is always thinking about something, and in the first instance it is thinking about something really present to it and one with it. It is self-consciousness before it is external perception or abstract discourse. Without the material presented in self-consciousness there would be no foundation for any other mode of thinking. But in self-consciousness, the reflective awareness of the sentient self, thinking is in the concrete inseparable from sentience. Hence we must extend to man what we have said of the animal psyche in general and hold that the human soul is a substantial form of the organism. Man is not simply a soul inhabiting a body but a substantial unity of body and soul.

In thus vindicating the Aristotelian conception of the soul as the form of the body, we need not, however, follow St. Thomas Aquinas in the theory in which he is almost alone among the chief medieval representatives of the Aristotelian tradition, and according to which the higher substantial forms absorb the lower, so that each substance has only one substantial form and the human soul immediately informs first matter. Aquinas, of course, had not the detailed scientific evidence about the persistence of the constituents within the chemical combination and of chemical molecules within living cells which make this theory highly unplausible for us in terms of experience. His motive seems to have been to insist on the natural unity of body and soul against any attempt to resurrect Platonism in Aristotelian terms by, for example, supposing a form of corporeity of the entire organism distinct from the cognitive principle or by distinguishing a sentient soul from the intellectual or spiritual soul.

On both these points he was surely right. The human soul is the only principle of unity of the entire organism and its mode of thinking is fundamentally one with its sentience. Nevertheless we may well think that unity of substance is analogical, so that the same thing may be at the same time one substance and many. As an experient being man is one, but there is nothing which forbids us to recognize the relative independence of living cells within that unity, of chemical molecules within the cell, of physical atoms within the molecule, and of the constituents of physical atoms themselves. This is what experience suggests, and the only metaphysical argument against it would be based on a univocal conception of the unity of substance which there seems to be no reason to uphold.

III

It is to be hoped that the foregoing exposition has shown that Thomistic man is not to be equated with Platonic or Cartesian man, and that the conception of the soul as the final substantial form of the body provides a more realistic basis for the discussion of human immortality by exhibiting where the difficulty lies. Death is neither a happy release of the soul from its imprisonment in matter nor the dissolution of a chance association; it is the destruction of a natural union. A human mind could not come into existence without a body, and the material for its thinking when embodied is provided through the agency of the body. If, then, we say that it is capable of existing and acting after ceasing to be embodied, we are making an assertion which is by no means obvious.

The classical argument for the survival of the mind or soul after death is based on the incorporeal character of thought. Since thinking is not a bodily activity, there is no reason why thinking and, consequently, also willing, should not continue in the absence of the body. Hence we may justifiably hold that we have an incorporeal kind of existence after death.

That thought is not corporeal, that it has no mass or dimensions, is evident enough to reflection, but we may wonder whether the foregoing argument does not prove too much. For sensations, considered apart from the bodily consciousness which accompanies them, are equally lacking in corporeal character. Should we attribute immortality to all sentient minds? Alternatively, if we take seriously the fact that sensations depend on bodily changes, must we not take equally seriously the fact that thought does not occur without sensation? If the former fact leads us to conclude that sentient minds do not survive the destruction of the body, must not the latter fact enforce the conclusion that thought does not persist without sensation and, consequently, perishes with the body also?

There is, however, an important difference between sensation and thought. The life of pure sensation acquires its whole significance from its relation to the organism; its drives are wholly directed to the preservation, development and propagation of the animal body. The life of thought, on the other hand, escapes the tyranny of the present moment to look backwards and forwards in time; it has a drive which is not exhausted by any finite time. Hence it is significant to hold that its energy persists after the dissolution of the body.

The argument for human immortality should, then, be supplemented by a consideration of the supratemporal significance of the life of thought. Thinking is not only an intrinsically incorporeal activity, but it is an activity whose drive is not exhausted by what it achieves during the life of the bodily organism. Hence we may justifiably hold that its energy continues after death.

But we have not solved the difficulty that, as sensation is dependent on the body, so thought as we know it is dependent on sensation. What can be, so to say, the stuff of experience after death? What corresponds with the role which sensation plays in our present existence?

This difficulty is rightly given prominence in what deserves to be called the most acute criticism of the Thomistic doctrine of immortality from within the Aristotelian tradition, the treatise of Pomponazzi (Pomponatius) *De Immortalitate Animae*, written in 1516. Pomponazzi agrees with St. Thomas in rejecting the Averroist theory of a separate and supra-individual active intellect. He also agrees with him in rejecting any theory of two souls in man, a perishable sentient soul and an immortal intellectual soul. Apart from more elaborate arguments, experience is enough to tell us that it is the individual self which both senses and thinks and that the sentient mind is one with the thinking mind.

Hence we may well say that the human mind, in so far as it is intellectual, participates in the character of immortal things, but can we say of a mind which is also sentient and the form of a bodily organism that it is itself literally immortal? We are faced with the difficulty put clearly by Aristotle himself; if thinking is either a sort of imagination or could not occur without imagination, it cannot exist without the body.[1] Pomponazzi agrees again that thinking is not merely a sort of imagination, but the difficulty persists that thinking does not occur without imagination or sentience. This seems to have deterred Aristotle himself from asserting personal immortality, and it makes Pomponazzi regard immortality as beyond the competence of philosophy to demonstrate.

This objection is not to be underestimated, but its force can be reduced if we reflect that it does not prove that thought has no object after death; it shows only that we are ignorant of what that object may be. We certainly cannot suppose that we survive death with our thinking powers intact but with nothing to think about, and we have no positive conception of what will provide the stimulus to the activity of thought. Religion comes to our aid to some extent, and not only by substituting an assurance of immortality for the bare philosophical conclusion that the life of thought is not of its nature such as to perish with death. It also leaves us in contact with reality after death, for we are always in relation to God. Apart from the thought of God death would seem to leave us without an environment, isolated from everything we know even if conceivably still existent. The religious man is content to leave the basis of his future experience and thinking to the disposition of his Creator. Even so, however, religion does not give us any detailed information about the psychological conditions of that experience. Life after death remains mysterious.

---

[1] Μάλιστα δ'ἔοικεν ἴδιον τὸ νοεῖν · εἰ δ'ἐστὶ καὶ τοῦτο φαντασία τις ἢ μὴ ἄνευ φαντασίας οὐκ ἐνδέχοιτ' ἂν οὐδὲ τοῦτ' ἄνευ σώματος εἶναι. (Aristotle: De Anima I i, 403a 8-10).

The other objection, also prominent in Pomponazzi's work, that it is contrary to the nature of a form to become a separate existent, is of a more purely systematic and less really impressive kind. It is true that to assert both that the soul is the form of the bodily organism and that it is immortal involves an analogical extension of the meaning of form which is unique and was apparently too much for Aristotle himself. But, if reflection demands it, this extension of meaning can be made without evacuating the complementary acknowledgment of the intimate unity of body and soul as we know them that is intended by the application of the categories of matter and form.

In sum, then, we are aware in our present experience of ourselves as thinking and sentient organisms, whose thought derives its material from sensation and whose sensations are dependent on bodily changes. We have thus a single nature in the Aristotelian sense of a unitary principle of activity, and the soul must be regarded in Aristotelian terms as the form of the body. Yet the life of thought is not only intrinsically incorporeal but has an impetus which transcends the day-by-day life of the organism and is conversant with what goes beyond space and time. Hence there is no intrinsic reason why it should cease with the destruction of the body. Philosophy cannot tell us the basis of experience after death, but it leaves us with the hope of an immortality which may gain positive assurance and content from religion. When we discuss man's moral development, we are discussing the proper activity of a being which is not doomed to rapid extinction but is capable both of conceiving and of affirming, with however much of mystery, a future beyond death.

Chapter III

MORAL EXPERIENCE

I

MORAL philosophy may be approached in more than one way. Aristotle's approach was to ask in what consisted the proper fulfilment of human nature. That is a question which must arise sooner or later, but it arises within a context, and it is best to leave it until we see why it has to be asked. Moreover, if it is put at the beginning, confusion may be caused between the desire of happiness and the sense of moral obligation. Although these are by no means unconnected, their difference needs to be seen first.

Kant's approach has the advantage of making this distinction at once and of being an analysis of moral experience. It should also commend itself to our contemporaries as an investigation of the special sense in which the word "ought" is used in ethical judgments. While Kant's general philosophy made the elaboration of his ethics unduly laborious, it is equally instructive both to examine his initial analysis and to see why its adequate continuation brings us back to the questions and answers of an older tradition.

In other than ethical contexts the word "ought" and its equivalents are used in dependence on a condition, and this condition is a dominant purpose. To say that you ought to do this or that is to suggest a useful or necessary means to an end. If I tell you that you ought to take golf lessons from the professional, I am assuming that you want to improve your golf. If I do not make this assumption, I shall express myself conditionally and say, "If you want to be a good golfer, you ought to take lessons from the professional." If I neither express the condition, nor have any ground for making the assumption, I am merely being impertinent. You will point out to me in reply that you have not the faintest desire to play golf at all and that, consequently, there is no "ought" about it.

Such, for Kant, is the problematic hypothetical imperative. It is hypothetical because it depends on a condition, and it is problematic because the condition is not necessarily fulfilled. There is, however, another sort of non-moral imperative which, although hypothetical, is not problematic but assertoric. The condition in this case is necessarily fulfilled, for it consists in the desire for happiness, and no man can really desire to be unhappy. The men who relish gloom and "enjoy" bad health do not wish to be unhappy but find a peculiar kind of happiness in what makes others unhappy.

Hence it is indifferent whether I say to you, "If you want to be happy, you ought to cut your losses and make the best of the present", or simply, "You ought to cut your losses and make the best of the present." If I say the latter and you ask why, it is enough to answer that you will not be happy unless you do so, and, if you retort that you have lost the desire to be happy, I have every right to come back with the statements that you are now finding a perverse kind of enjoyment in brooding over the past, that this will not make you content in the end, and that you will only find the real happiness you desire if you get out of this mood.

Both these kinds of conditional "ought" are different from the categorical or unconditional imperative of morality. This is an "ought" because it is not necessarily fulfilled, but it is unconditional because it holds whether it subserves my purposes or conflicts with them. If I am told that I ought to be honest in my dealings, it is no answer to object that I want to make money and that I can do so by means of a dishonest trick. The point is simply that I ought to be honest, whether it be in this case the best policy or not.

Kant is so anxious to make a sharp distinction between the categorical imperative of morality and anything considered as a means to an end that he sometimes exaggerates the absence of desire in a moral act and the complete disinterestedness with which it is to be performed. Of course there must be the specific desire to fulfil our moral obligations, or else no one would ever fulfil them, and it is all to the good if our other desires are such as to harmonize with this. Moreover it may well be true, and we may well acknowledge, that the fulfilment of duty leads to happiness in the end. Kant, indeed, was as insistent as any philosopher that the universe would be irrational if morality and happiness did not eventually coincide. What he is really asking us to do is not to confuse the question whether the fulfilment of duty in fact leads to happiness with the question whether the moral imperative presents itself precisely as a means to happiness.

When we interrogate moral experience for the answer to the latter question, we must surely agree with Kant. What I recognize as moral obligations are such that I see myself as bound to fulfil them whatever the consequences may be. If I thought of my duty as standing or falling with the ulterior consequences to myself, I should not be thinking in a fully ethical way. There remains a distinction between moral principle as such and even the most enlightened self-interest.

The same point may be expressed by saying that we ought to do our duty for duty's sake, but this formula is somewhat ambiguous. It might sound as if duty were some final end beyond the dutiful action itself, but the real intention is precisely to deny that we need look beyond the dutiful action as such for the source of its obligatory character. It might suggest also that an action is not dutiful unless its formal character of obligatoriness is what moves us to do it. Kant evidently takes this to be the case. But the motive is really the same if it is considered materially as, say, an act of kindness or an act of justice. To imply that I am not acting in a fully dutiful way if I do something because it is an act of kindness to you without explicitly reflecting that it is my duty to be kind to you is absurd. It is like saying that I cannot reason correctly unless I reflect on the figure and mood of the syllogism that I am employing. Here Kant betrays his excessive formalism.

We can sum this up in another way under the head of motive. The motive of choice is not to be thought of as something other than what is chosen in its totality, but it is the factor in what is chosen which moves the agent to choose it. We act rightly when we do what is in fact right from a right motive. To tell the truth for fear of being despised as a liar is to do what is in fact one's duty, but it is not to do it as one's duty, because the motive is less than worthy. But, when we tell the truth because we acknowledge truth-telling as something which obliges us, we are acting rightly without needing to reflect formally on the character of obligation in general. Right action is all the better for being spontaneous.

II

We must now widen our view of the moral situation, for morality is not exclusively a matter of the recognition and fulfilment of absolute imperatives. Besides the sense of right in which it means "obligatory", there is the sense in which it means "morally permissible" and the sense in which it means "morally desirable".

For moral obligation and moral perfection are not identical. Too many philosophers, including Kant, have written as if it were always obligatory to do the best possible act in the circumstances. But this is contrary to our moral consciousness and would impose an intolerable burden on human nature. In ordinary circumstances we recognize a certain standard below which we must not fall; the choice of the better is laudable but not strictly obligatory.

Thus it is right, in the sense of obligatory, not to deceive anyone who asks us for information which there is no peremptory
reason for withholding; to mislead him would be morally wrong.
But there is no obligation to give the fullest possible information
to every inquirer; it is right, in the sense of permissible, to
answer him truthfully without communicating everything that
he might conceivably wish to know. Yet it is also right, in the
sense of morally desirable, to take the trouble to enlighten him
as fully as we usefully can.

There are also situations in which, when the demands of strict
moral obligation have been satisfied, there is no one course of
action which is the best possible. Hence, even if we are looking
for moral perfection, we are still left with freedom of choice.
There being no reason why I should fast, I am perfectly free
morally to choose beef or mutton from the menu, claret or
burgundy from the wine list. This is a relatively trivial instance,
but life would be rather dull if there were not a sufficient number
of cases in which even the demands of moral perfection did not
leave one free to make a completely spontaneous choice. Otherwise life would be, in a moral sense, all work and no play.

The moral philosopher has, therefore, to take account not only
of the morally obligatory but also of the morally permissible and
the morally desirable. It is Kant's exclusive concentration on the
categorical imperative, as well as his rigorism in difficult cases,
which gives to his moral philosophy an air of excessive puritan-
ism. No doubt it is often difficult to draw the line where strict
obligation ceases, but ethical reflection should help to do this as
well as to make clear what our absolute obligations are.

III

When Kant asked himself what could be the content of a categorical imperative, he had to face the difficulties created by the
theory of knowledge which he had previously elaborated in the

Critique of Pure Reason. If everything empirical was merely phenomenal, he had to exclude the empirical from his fundamental ethical principles, for he wanted to assert the absolute and independent validity of morality. To this embarrassment is due the tortuous development of thought which is presented in different ways in the *Foundation of the Metaphysic of Morals* and in the *Critique of the Practical Reason.*

First of all, then, Kant concludes from the principle that duty is to be done for duty's sake that we should so act that we can at the same time will that the maxim of our action should become a universal law or as if, by so acting, we made our maxim into a universal law. He gives as an example that, when we are tempted to make a false promise, we might do so if we thought only of our own advantage, but we cannot desire that everyone should act in this way. For that would entail the end of all mutual trust, and promises would become meaningless, our own included. Thus, as a universal principle, the maxim on which we are inclined to make a false promise is self-destructive.

Kant's conclusion is here more admirable than his argument. For an imperative is not necessarily a simple application of a universal law. A sound moral judgment has, indeed, to be careful to take account of particular circumstances in particular cases. Duty for duty's sake, therefore, does not mean acting from reverence for universal law but doing your particular duty here and now because it is your duty here and now. The note of universality is surreptitiously introduced, and sounds plausible only because so much of right action has the character of obedience to general laws. If Kant's conclusion is acceptable, it is not on account of his argument but because morality demands that the claims of self and of others should be treated equally. We cannot morally approve of doing to others what we should not approve of their doing to us in a like case.

Kant goes on to say that, if duty is not a means to an end, it must derive its validity from something which is an end in itself. If duty is absolute, it must be based on something of absolute value. This can only be the personal dignity of rational human nature itself. Hence the categorical imperative now commands us so to act as to use humanity, both in ourselves and in others, always as an end and never merely as a means.

Here again the conclusion is better than the argument. Our fundamental human equality is once more the ground on which we should never treat others merely as means to our private ends. But it does not follow from the principle of duty for duty's sake that we or our rational nature or our moral perfection are absolutes and ends in themselves from every point of view. It is true only that, in doing our duty, it is enough to know that it is our duty, and we need not look for any further motive or purpose for doing it.

It is evident, then, that Kant's difficulty is the result of his general philosophy. Since he regards the nature of things as they are in themselves as hidden from us, he has to try to give a content to the categorical imperative by manipulating its formal character without recourse to empirical fact. It is not remarkable that the effort should be unsuccessful. With a different general philosophy we can now take leave of Kant and look for the basis of duty in the nature of things.

Previously, however, we must take note that in some sense "ought" implies "can". It would be useless to tell a man that he ought to do something unless he was able to do it. A moral act, therefore, is one which we can do or forbear to do. We must ask, therefore, in what sense the moral "ought" implies "can", and in what sense or senses we are able to choose what we do. This is the problem of free will.

Chapter IV

FREE WILL AND RIGHT ACTION

I

Few features of human nature have been so unkindly treated by philosophers as free will. Many thinkers tell us that our belief in free will is a delusion, and of those who admit its validity and try to explain what it means many end by offering us something very unlike what free will seems to be in experience. The difficulty of the question is not to be under-rated.

Yet we are pointing not to a remote conclusion but to something in experience when we talk about free will. We feel ourselves to be masters of at least some of our actions in a way which is not applicable to a dog or a cat, and still less to any non-sentient or any inanimate object. We feel morally responsible for some at least of what we do or forbear to do, and moral responsibility is an ultimate personal responsibility which we cannot throw off on anything else or on an unchanging order of the whole universe. Praise and blame, reward and punishment, have a different and sharpened meaning as applied to men from the meaning which they have as applied to anything else. These are aspects of experience which cannot easily be explained away.

If we examine first what Aristotle says about free will at the beginning of the third book of the *Nicomachean Ethics*, we shall see what was made of the question by a great philosopher who approached it freshly without the doubtful benefit of all the muddles introduced by later thinkers. Not that Aristotle's discussion is entirely unmuddled, but his muddles are only the vaguenesses of a first attempt to deal with a highly complex problem. We may agree with Sir David Ross when he writes, "On the whole we must say that he shared the plain man's belief in free will but that he did not examine the problem very thoroughly, and did not express himself with perfect consistency."[1] Nevertheless Aristotle's treatment is a good introduction to the subject, for he kept close to experience and said nothing obviously false or in collision with the facts.

Aristotle begins by trying to determine the sphere of what should be described as ἑκούσιον, a word which, as he uses it, is better translated as "spontaneous" than as "voluntary", in a sense in which "spontaneous" is wider than "voluntary" but does not exclude it. For it is applicable to every action which is an expression of a conscious tendency of the agent even though it may not be under his control. It excludes, however, actions which are literally forced upon you, as when you are carried off by bandits. In a sense you make the movements, but they are certainly not an expression of your desire.

In a less strict sense we speak of being forced to do things when we do them for fear of a worse alternative. Such is the action of a captain who throws valuable cargo overboard during a storm in order to lighten the ship and save his own life and the lives of the crew. The act is unwelcome, but in the circumstances it is preferred. Since actions have to be judged in their full concreteness, such an act must be recognized as an expression of the prevalent desire at the time and so is not excluded from the range of the spontaneous.

The same cannot be said of an act done through ignorance. In the measure that you are ignorant of the nature of your act, or of its circumstances, or of its effects, you cannot be held responsible for it. It is true that your ignorance may itself be culpable; if you are violent because you are drunk, you are not thereby excused, and your actions may be said to be performed in ignorance rather than through ignorance. Nevertheless it is for

[1] W. D. Ross, *Aristotle*, London, 1930, p. 201.

your ignorance in conjunction with its effects that you are responsible, rather than for the effects in isolation.

A spontaneous act, therefore, is one which is neither forced on the agent nor done through ignorance; it is an expression of his conscious tendency. But we must take a step farther in order to reach the kind of act which is ethically significant, for a merely spontaneous act is not necessarily under our control and may be performed quite automatically. Infants and animals act spontaneously, but their acts lack an ethical character because they are not the result of deliberate choice. What is voluntary in the full sense of the term is a choice.

The situation of choice cannot be described in purely conative terms. If we consider only the element of passion or desire or wish, we have not got what precisely makes a choice. Still less, of course, is choice purely cognitive. It is only too clear that we may believe an object to be good or an act to be right without choosing to pursue the object or to perform the act. The situation of choice is one in which both the cognitive and the conative factors must be taken into account; it is a spontaneous act which follows on deliberation.

The field of choice, then, is limited by the possibility of deliberation. But, says Aristotle, we do not deliberate about events of which the issue is already certain, nor do we deliberate about events whose issue we have no conception how to affect. We deliberate only about things which are, or are thought to be, within our control. Nor, when we have decided what we want and how to get it, do we deliberate any longer. We deliberate about what is not yet determinate in itself and what we have not yet determined to bring about. Hence the determination is thought of as coming from us. Choice is regarded as depending on ourselves.

Actions are called virtuous or vicious when they are the result of choice and in accordance with whether the choice is right or wrong. Hence virtue and vice are voluntary and chosen and depend on ourselves. We are able to say "Yes" or "No", and we are responsible for the answer. This conclusion is supported not only by individual experience but by the social system of rewards and punishments, which presupposes that men are responsible for making themselves virtuous or vicious. Crimes done in ignorance are punished when the offender is held to be responsible for his ignorance and not otherwise.

Aristotle was not unacquainted with the point of view which we would call psychological determinism. He puts to himself the objection that, although a man makes choices which are genuinely his own, they are the result of his character. He answers that his moral character consists largely of habits which are the outcome of past choices and so must be laid to his account. A man cannot throw off his habits at will, it is true, but he might have avoided acquiring them. But what of innate qualities of character? Aristotle has nothing very clear to say on this point, but he clings to the experienced fact of responsibility both for virtue and for vice.

So far Aristotle. While we still need a discrimination of kinds of choice and an analysis of the causal structure of the situation of choice, the main facts to which we have to do justice are fairly set out in his discussion.

II

Hobbes wrote a short book which hardly lives up to its long title: *Of Liberty and Necessity, a Treatise wherein all Controversy concerning Predestination, Election, Free-will, Grace, Merits, Reprobation, etc. is fully decided and cleared*. Here he seeks to defend determinism by showing that all the facts which are commonly thought to need an explanation in terms of free will can be reasonably interpreted without it.

> The law regardeth the will and no other precedent causes of action ... What necessary cause soever precede an action, yet, if the action be forbidden, he that doth it willingly may

justly be punished ... To make the law is therefore to make a cause of justice and to necessitate justice; and consequently 'tis no injustice to make such a law ... What is it else to praise but to say a thing is good? ... And what is it to say an action is good but to say it is as I would wish? Or as another would have it, or according to the will of the state? ... Things may be therefore necessary and yet praiseworthy, as also necessary and yet dispraised, and neither of them both in vain, because praise and dispraise, and likewise reward and punishment, do by example make and conform the will to good and evil.[1]

These contentions, which were echoed in less picturesque language by J. S. Mill two centuries later, must be held to miss the point. It is quite true that praise and blame, and that laws, with rewards and punishments, would have an intelligible purpose even if the will were not free, but the question is rather whether, as applied to an adult human being, they have no more than the significance which Hobbes allows them. We should admit that they have a meaning of their own as applied to a responsible adult.

Praise of a good man is very different from praise of a good piece of workmanship, and praise of a virtuous action is very different even from praise of a sharp understanding. A moral judgment is directed in a special way to a man's individual personality; his virtues and vices are thought to belong to him in an even more intimate way than his intellectual powers. Moral praise is more than praise in general, and blame more than dispraise in general. We do not blame a chair for collapsing under us, but we do blame a man for betraying the trust we reposed in him. For the man could have helped it; the chair could not.

Reward and punishment, in the same way, have a different significance as applied to infants and animals and as applied to a responsible adult. Indeed, it might be better not to use the same terms at all when we refer to necessary methods of training

[1] Thomas Hobbes, Of Liberty and Necessity, ed. of 1684 in Hobbs's Tripos, pp. 287-91.

animals or even the growing human being. We know that the dog could not and cannot make himself other than he is. What praise or blame we give him does not finally rest on this individual dog; we look for the entire source of his qualities, good and bad, in his pedigree and physique, his previous environment and training. Whatever training we give him should be eventually for his good as well as for our own.

Premature moralizing can be even more harmful to the young than plain corporal punishment, with regard to which they are usually gifted with considerable resilience. The rod remains a useful form of conditioning for the young precisely when it is treated as such and employed with a mixture of realism and good temper. It is when a man matures and can be expected to have an adequate recognition of the rightness of right and the wrongness of wrong that reward and punishment acquire their full meaning. Then they are deserved. It is his own fault, we say, he has brought it on himself, he has only himself to blame. When a man's wrongdoing can be traced to circumstances or upbringing or heredity, we pity but we do not blame. Such a man may have to be restrained for his own good or for the sake of society, but the opinion of mankind makes a clear distinction between this case and that in which no adequate excuse can be found, where the wrongdoer is himself the source of his wrongdoing and deserves the consequences of his actions. No doubt the motive of punishment continues to be reformation or deterrence, for human judgment is incapable of assessing the proper measure of retribution, but the necessary foundation of punishment in the full sense of the term is a deserving which presupposes some ultimate personal responsibility.

An objection to free will of the type made by Hobbes fails because it does not acknowledge the essential difference between praise and blame, reward and punishment, as applied to a moral agent and as applied to anything else. A theory which makes no difference between moral judgments and other judgments of value is an evident falsification of the facts. The basis of the difference consists in moral responsibility. We have not yet tried to explain this positively, but it is not difficult to see that it must have a special kind of analysis.

III

There is, no doubt, a sense in which free and responsible choice is equated with deliberate choice. When a decision is not the result of being carried away by the impulse of the moment but springs from our weighing of the alternatives, it is in a special way our own. That we often use the term *free* in this sense is evident. This is, indeed, as far as Aristotle's analysis went, and it sufficed the medieval Aristotelians for their account of moral freedom.

But can it be the only sense in which we speak of choosing freely? For freedom in this sense is not incompatible with an ultimate determinism. There are plenty of cases in which only one alternative appears reasonable after deliberation, and consequently we are certain to choose it. If I look at the weather outside and see that rain is imminent, I shall infallibly take my umbrella out with me. The only sense in which I can be said to act freely apart from my having previously deliberated is that, if I was mad or enjoyed getting wet or had too many other things to carry, I should not take the umbrella. But these hypotheses are not verified; in the circumstances I cannot choose otherwise than as I do.

In other cases there is at least an appearance of greater freedom because an onlooker is insufficiently acquainted with the character of the agent. Will this man give me the help I need? I do not know, but it may be that he is really the sort of man who will certainly do so. This unfailing kindness, it may well be said, is a habit of goodness which is due to past free choices. Then we ask in what sense the original choices were free. Unless they were free in a sense fuller than that of being merely deliberate, we should still be able with an ideally complete knowledge to account for all human actions in terms of innate character, circumstances and training.

If this were true, the sense of moral responsibility would ultimately be a delusion, for we could always assert in the end that we could not have chosen otherwise than as we did choose. But we feel morally responsible precisely when we are unable to account for our actions without invoking critical decisions which, although all the relevant factors are considered, might have been other than what they were. It is to the extent that we have made ourselves what we are, and have not been made by anything other than ourselves or even by our innate character to choose as we did, that we feel morally responsible for what we are. In the Aristotelian tradition the need of this further sense of freedom was first emphasized by the sixteenth-century thinker Molina.

Hence we cannot account for moral responsibility by merely adding to the factor of deliberate choice the power to do as we choose. This is the important sense of freedom in a political context, but it is not moral freedom of choice. Nevertheless Locke asks us to be content with this sort of freedom.

> So far as a man has power to think or not to think, to move or not to move, according to the preference or direction of his own mind; so far is a man free.[1]

On this assumption the question whether a man's will be free or not becomes "unreasonable because unintelligible". Liberty is one power and will is another; one does not belong to the other, but both belong to the man. Will is the power of choosing a course of action, and liberty is the power of acting in accordance with choice. Consequently "the question is not proper whether the will be free, but whether a man be free."

Professor Moore does not really add anything of importance when he says:

[1] John Locke, *Essay Concerning Human Understanding*, bk ii, ch. xxi, §8.

(1) that we often *should* have *acted* differently if we had chosen to; (2) that similarly we often should have *chosen* differently, *if* we had chosen so to choose; and (3) that it was almost always *possible* that we should have chosen differently, in the sense that no man could know for certain that we should *not* so choose.[1]

The first point is simple liberty to do as we choose; on the second point Moore allows it to be supposed that we are determined to choose so to choose; on the third the ignorance of our motives on the part of others is no argument against those motives in fact determining our choice.

Really there can be no doubt that what we are seeking in order to make moral responsibility intelligible is nothing subsequent to the choice but a special freedom in the actual choosing. Locke comes nearer to acknowledging this in another passage:

> The mind having in most cases, as is evident in experience, a power to suspend the execution and satisfaction of any of its desires, and so all, one after another, is at liberty to consider the objects of them, examine them on all sides, and weigh them with others. In this lies the liberty man has.[2]

A power to suspend the pressure of desire is also a power to cease suspending it, which is to come to a decision in favour of the desire which is uppermost at that moment. This at any rate suggests what we are looking for, but does not explain how we have such a power or how it comes into play.

IV

The difficulty, as it presents itself at this stage of the discussion, is well analysed by Professor Broad. While determinism is clearly

---

[1] G. E. Moore, *Ethics*, London, 1930, p. 220.
[2] Locke, *Human Understanding*, bk. ii, ch. xxi, §47.

incompatible with moral responsibility, an element of indeterminism in the sequence of events can hardly be distinguished from chance or accident. What we want to be able to assert is that the choice is made "*by the agent or self*, considered as a substance or continuant".[1] Since Broad finds this unintelligible, he is left doubting whether the notion of moral obligation has any application.

Broad might be thought a little hasty at this point in ignoring Kant's theory of moral freedom. However unacceptable it may be as it stands, it is a doctrine of the kind which he regards as needful if sense is to be made of moral obligation, and Kant's mistakes are usually of the variety which repays examination. For Kant the succession of events in time is both merely phenomenal and such as demands to be brought under laws of causal determination. Hence it is doubly useless to look for moral freedom in the world of objective experience. This does not reveal things as they are in themselves, and we can master it only by seeing it in terms of determining cause and determined effect.

Freedom is to be found in the moral will acknowledging the categorical imperative. There an ambiguity occurs. Is the moral will always a fully rational will? Much of what Kant says implies that this is the case. If so, the moral will is free in the sense of being exempt from irrational or unworthy motives; it is essentially above mere impulse, desire or passion. Hence, when the moral will comes into play, it will not only infallibly recognize the categorical imperative but it will infallibly obey it. Moral freedom is a freedom from the possibility of evil, not a freedom to choose between good and evil. But wrongdoing is a fact. We are faced with the problem why the moral will does not always assert itself and how we become victims of the amoral, or in this case immoral, determinism of the world of phenomena. Kant does not give us an answer.

On other occasions Kant seems to be taking the commonsense

---

[1] C. D. Broad, "Determinism, Indeterminism, and Libertarianism", in *Ethics and the History of Philosophy*, London, 1952, p. 214.

view that moral freedom in this stage of existence is a power of choice between good and evil. The moral will is as responsible for evil as it is for good. Now the question is how the moral will, which is in some sense a rational will, can at times be an immoral and an irrational will. Again Kant leaves us in perplexity. All that we can retain from him is the need of looking for a kind of causality different from the relation between determining antecedents and determined consequents.

We cannot get any farther with Bradley, who tells us that we have a "true self" which manifests itself in right acts, but leaves in obscurity why this true self is in some cases so fitfully effective. The recent Russian thinker Nicolai Lossky, although unduly influenced by idealist terminology, comes nearer to an integrated view of the causality involved in ethical action.[1] The world of events in space and time, considered by itself, could only be thought of as determined by laws of succession. But it cannot be accounted for in isolation, for change has its real source in the interrelatedness of substantial agents. Man is such an agent, and his power of choice is an ultimate freedom to select one alternative or another and so to make himself for good or evil.

This may be asserted a good deal more clearly on the basis of a wholeheartedly realist metaphysic. Modern difficulties on the subject go back to the failure of eighteenth-century philosophers to consider causality except under the aspect of laws of succession in time. Against this limited conception of causality Hume could make pertinent objections, and Kant was unable to rehabilitate it as more than a category in terms of which we could not help thinking of the field of phenomena. Plainly this cannot be the whole story, for, as Russell and Collingwood have pointed out in our own day, if causality were confined to what we take to be laws of succession, then, since cause and effect must be simultaneous, everything would happen at once. Thus causality as a mere order of succession contradicts itself.

The remedy is not, like Russell and Collingwood, to give up

[1] Cf. N. O. Lossky, *Freedom of Will*, London, 1932, esp. ch. vi.

causality as a bad job, but to enlarge its conception in a way adequate to our experience and thinking. Sudden changes can be thought of only as conclusions of processes of continuous change, and such processes have their source in the relations of things which persist in time, that is to say, of substances. Substances themselves, as maintaining their essential identity through changes of attribute and activity, must be thought of as causally related in an immanent way to their own changing attributes and activities. Causality becomes intelligible when it is considered, first, as the immanent simultaneous agency of those unities of potentiality which we call substances to their own actual states and activities; secondly, as the transeunt simultaneous causality which is the source of continuous change among things in their interrelatedness; and thirdly, as manifesting itself in the succession of discrete changes which arise out of causality in the former two senses. Gas, having been put into a state of ignition, gradually warms the water in the kettle until the water boils. However more elaborately a scientist might analyse this process, the threefold pattern of causality must be preserved in order to make the account intelligible.[1]

For the purpose of an analysis of free will we must go back behind that event in time which is a choice, with its antecedent desire and deliberation, to the agent of which the choice is an act. We must ask in what special way the act must come from the agent in order to make him morally responsible for it. Our main objective thus finally discloses itself.

V

Deliberation does not involve freedom of choice in the full sense, for it may reveal only one course of action which has any attraction for us in the end. Here deliberation determines decision, and

[1] For a justification of this general doctrine of causality cf. my *Being and Becoming*, London, 1954, chs. vii–viii, x–xii.

the deliberation itself was determined by our character and circumstances, but what about the case in which reflection leaves us still with rival claims or attractions? In such a case Buridan's ass is said to have died of hunger, unable to make up its mind between two equally satisfying bundles of hay. A man would be even more of an ass if he allowed himself to suffer the fate of this legendary animal.

Such a case may be made to sound too rare if we talk of equal attractions. There is no mathematical equality in these matters. The case is one in which no possible course of action is so overwhelmingly attractive as to cancel the attraction of the other or of others. How do we make up our minds? When we consider merely successive causation, we are inclined to answer that one attraction must prove overwhelmingly strong in the end. Otherwise the choice would seem to be mere chance, accident or caprice, and we are rightly reluctant to admit absolute chance. In any case it would have nothing to do with moral values.

The situation looks different when we take into account simultaneous immanent causality or agency. The choice is always an act of the agent, but sometimes the antecedents determine it to be an act of a certain kind. When they leave the issue open, they provide the conditions under which the final choice proceeds exclusively from the free causality of the agent as such. But surely, we may say, in such a case the decision is determined by the character of the agent. No, for we are no longer concerned with a causal relation on the level of determinate actuality; we are concerned with the causal relation of a power to its act. When both the nature of the power itself and the circumstances in which it operates leave the issue open, the power actualizes itself freely in the full sense of the term. The agent is ultimately responsible for its act and cannot throw the responsibility back on anything else or even on its own nature.

It is determined that a choice should be made. For, even if we are thinking of a choice between A, B and C, this can be broken down into choices between A and not-A, B and not-B, C and not-C. It is logically necessary that we should choose between A and not-A. Any choice we make is motivated, for there is motive both for A and for not-A, whether the motive in the latter case be directly for not-A or for the incompatible alternatives B and C. But, with this balance of motives, the direction of the choice is not determined. The actual choice is not, however, an irrational coming-to-be of something out of nothing but the exclusive self-actualization of the agent. This explains the unique personal responsibility which we feel for such choices.

Nevertheless a choice which is fully free in this sense is not necessarily of moral importance. It may be that I have no overwhelming motive to travel by train rather than omnibus or to eat beef rather than mutton. That we can often exercise free choice without incurring moral praise or blame is a satisfaction to our spontaneity which is not to be despised, but free will would hardly deserve all this discussion unless it commonly possessed moral moment.

As far as the connection between free will and ethics is concerned, Aristotle already had the root of the matter in him when he said that "there are three things which lead to choice and three which lead to avoidance: the noble, the expedient and the pleasant, and their contraries, the base, the harmful and the painful."[1] The attraction exerted by these different kinds of good and the repulsion exerted by their contraries are themselves of different kinds. The pleasant is the immediate good corresponding with my present impulse; the expedient is the means to my future good; the noble is the absolutely good when everything relevant is considered. Since men are individuals who are distinct and whose existence is spread over time, they are not moved exclusively by the absolutely good. My personal advantage has an attraction for me which is of a different kind from the attraction of what is absolutely good, and my present pleasure makes a special appeal which may be in opposition to my future advantage as well as to the absolutely good. There may, therefore,

[1] Aristotle, *Nicomachean Ethics*, II iii, 1104 b 30.

be an irreducible opposition of motives of mere pleasure or of personal advantage and of motives of absolute goodness, and this is the situation of moral free choice. Right action is that which is done for the sake of the noble, τοῦ καλοῦ ἕνεκα.

Thus moral choice involves a disparity of ends, which arises from the completeness or partiality of the goods which solicit the will. The extreme instance of partiality is the often violent impulse to immediate pleasure. In so far as the agent takes his own future into account, and still more as he considers the good of others affected by his action, he transcends the limitations of immediate impulse, but, since he remains an individual existing in time, the special pressure of immediate impulse is not cancelled. Hence it is with greater or less difficulty that he learns both to enlarge the ambit of his consideration and to choose what does not ignore his own good but harmonizes it in the comprehensive good of all affected by what he does. This analysis seems to be consonant with our moral experience.

VI

The objections commonly made to free will in the full sense of the term are less difficult to repel than their frequent repetition might suggest. Sometimes a rigid principle of causality is invoked. Everything that comes to be is causally determined by its antecedents, and this applies to volitions as much as to anything else. Hence, while we may be ignorant of the causes of some volitions, they must have causes. A genuinely free choice is a metaphysical impossibility.

It is enough to reply that this principle of causality is a myth. That everything that comes to be is caused in some sense and in some way is doubtless true, but that it is always strictly determined by temporal antecedents is an entirely gratuitous assertion. The analysis of free will shows that, while a fully free choice is antecedently motivated, it is not antecedently determined. What is determined is precisely that there should be a choice and that the choice should be the free self-actualization of the agent. Consequently the objection simply begs the question which it is intended to argue.

Since Hume's assault on the metaphysics of causality this objection has usually been differently expressed. Whatever may be thought, we are told, of the metaphysical status of causality, experience shows that human conduct is just as capable of being brought under general laws as anything else. Regular sequences are observed alike in the material world and in human behaviour. Hence there is no ground for attributing a freedom to the will which does not belong to the objects of physical science. This form of objection has been expressed by Hume himself, by Mill and more recently, for example, by Bertrand Russell.

In this connection it must be recalled that not all volitions are free in the full sense of the term and that, where there is full freedom of choice, it is always freedom within a certain range of possibilities sometimes wider, sometimes narrower. Consequently there is plenty of room for probable and approximate generalizations about human conduct. Our position would be affected only if all conduct could be brought under exact general laws and if it were always true that, with complete knowledge of the antecedent situation, human choices could be predicted with certainty. There is no ground at all for making such assertions. Indeed, it is notoriously more difficult to arrive even at probable generalizations about human behaviour than about physical events, and generalizations about human behaviour appear to wear an approximate character on the face of them. We are entitled, after analysing free will, to assign the special freedom of human choice as the ground of this difference. The difference in availability of generalization between the physical and the human sciences is a point in favour of free will.

Still less need be said about the objection which identifies free choice in the full sense with chance or caprice. This is an elementary confusion of undetermined action with unmotivated action. Although fully free choice is not antecedently determined, there is motive for whatever choice is made. Hence it is not irrational or fortuitous but is precisely the kind of action which proceeds most completely from the self as agent and for which the self is fully responsible.

VII

In the course of this chapter we have distinguished several senses of freedom. Freedom to do as we choose depends not on ourselves but on circumstances. Consequently, moral obligation is not strictly to do this or that, but rather to do all in our power to bring something about. As H. A. Prichard put it, "an obligation must be an obligation not to do something but to set ourselves to do something."[1] There he was, probably unconsciously, echoing Abelard's insistence that the whole moral factor is reducible to the consent of the will.[2] It is convenient in practice, however, to take this refinement for granted and to speak simply of our obligation to do this or that.

What we may call freedom of deliberation is compatible with an ultimate determinism. Full freedom of choice belongs only to decisions in which there is a persistent conflict of alternatives. The kind of choice in which the alternatives are of widely different character and effect, and in which after a desperate struggle we yield ourselves with full consciousness to one side or the other, is comparatively rare. The necessity of making such a choice is a moral crisis. Yet on many occasions there is a certain range of indeterminacy, and we are constantly making ourselves, for better or for worse, a little different from what we might have been. Besides, every action tends either to contribute to the

[1] H. A. Prichard, "Duty and Ignorance of Fact", reprinted in *Moral Obligation*, Oxford, 1949, p. 35.
[2] Cf. Peter Abelard, *Scito Teipsum*, ch. iii.

formation of a habit, or to increase or reduce the strength of one which has already been acquired, so that it affects the range of indeterminacy within which choice will operate in the future. So, in the end, we are responsible for a considerable part of what we are. That is why the law can justifiably regard us as responsible for all our deliberate acts unless reason can be shown to the contrary.

Nevertheless, if we were to try to assess accurately whether and how far a man is ultimately responsible for some particular action, we should have to take into account all the factors of nature, upbringing and circumstance which limited his choice. This is not a task which it is possible to face with confidence. The assessment of responsibility is difficult enough in our own case, and, unless we hold a position which compels us to attempt it, it is only reasonable to renounce the effort in the case of others.

The possession of freedom of choice is precious, because it enables a man to contribute to the making of himself what he is to become. Yet, since it carries with it the power to do evil as well as the power to do good, this kind of freedom is not a final good. The final good is a freedom from evil in which the choice of good becomes habitual, but which, since it is the outcome of right free choice in the past, is a flowering of the personality and not a constraint upon it. The development of the moral life is an effort to draw nearer to this ideal.

Chapter V

THE BASIS OF OBLIGATION

I

IT IS not difficult to see that the sense of moral obligation is a distinctive kind of acknowledgment which cannot be analysed into non-ethical terms. Yet we do not on this account have to say that we just happen to experience obligations of various sorts and that to seek any further explanation would involve us in the naturalistic fallacy, the mistake of trying to break down the distinctively ethical into non-ethical elements. Explanation can reasonably be sought by asking in what kind of situation the acknowledgment of moral obligation appears. It may be that a necessary connection of the synthetic type will then be revealed.

Hobbes is the master of those who hold that moral notions are merely a gloss on a fundamental and persistent egoism.

> But whatsoever is the object of any man's appetite or desire, that is it which he for his part calleth *good*; and the object of his hate and aversion, *evil*; and of his contempt, *vile* and *inconsiderable*. For these words of good, evil and contemptible, are ever used with relation to the person that useth them: there being nothing simply and absolutely so; nor any common rule of good and evil, to be taken from the nature of the objects themselves.[1]

Hence the primitive state of man would be a war of each against all, each seeking to gratify his own desires without regard to his

[1] Thomas Hobbes, *Leviathan*, ch. vi.

47

neighbour. But such a state of insecurity would defeat the egoism which was its source. Hence a more enlightened sense of self-interest leads us to concede those rights to others which our own good requires that they should acknowledge in us. Men enter into society by agreeing to respect one another's desires to the extent that is needed in order that each should attain the greatest gratification of his own desires on the whole.

Thus the fundamental principle of morals and law is "that men perform their covenents made".[1] Just as the law in particular cases enforces on men the fulfilment of their agreements on this matter or that, so the basic laws of human society enforce the agreements without which society could not exist at all. But it is always in the end our own interest which induces us either to recognize the basic human rights of others or to fulfil our specific agreements. We do so because under any other conditions our desires would, on the whole, be less fully gratified.

The impression produced by Hobbes is evident by way of reaction in the care with which the British moralists of the eighteenth century seek to show that benevolence is as natural an impulse as self-love But it is also evident in their attempts to strengthen their position by finding some sort of derivation for benevolence in self-love and by showing that benevolence and self-love do not conflict. Hume would like to say that sympathy makes us feel the good and evil fortune of others as if they were our own, and even Butler is anxious to display benevolence as ministering to a cool, as opposed to a passionate, self-love.

One might be inclined to answer Hume in the words of La Rochefoucauld: "Nous avons tous assez de force pour supporter les maux d'autrui." Perhaps, however, that goes too far, for love in its fullest sense imparts a real community of feeling. But love in that sense is neither a duty nor even a possibility towards the vast majority of other people, whereas moral obligations towards others are of far more frequent occurrence. We certainly cannot let their fulfilment depend on the existence of a quite

[1] Hobbes, ch. xv.

exceptional degree of sympathy. The force of benevolence as a
moral motive cannot be a mere sympathetic extension of feeling.

We must concede to Butler that the fulfilment of duty is, and
rightly is, a source of satisfaction to the agent, but it is at least
equally clear that this satisfaction is not the motive of right moral
action. We do not admire a man who acts in order that he may
have the pleasure of applauding himself, whatever objective
benefits he may confer on others. It remains that the moral force
of the motive of benevolence must be upheld in independence of
the motive of self-love.

In general, then, in answer to Hobbes and to any less down-
right attempt to reduce morality to egoism, we must say that
there is a clearly experienced difference of meaning between the
sense of duty and the desire for happiness. Even if we add a
qualification and speak of our deepest happiness or our ultimate
happiness, the difference of meaning subsists. If right action did
not lead to the agent's happiness, it would not be any less right
to do it. If we could really secure our happiness by doing wrong,
the wrong would not be any less wrong. Consequently we must
look beyond even enlightened self-interest for the basis of
obligation.

II

Among those who tried to answer Hobbes it would appear,
therefore, that they were more happily inspired who insisted on
the original and independent force of the motive of benevolence
and on the disinterested nature of virtuous action. Hutcheson
asserts the principle that the "actions our moral sense would most
recommend to our election as the most perfectly virtuous" are
"such as appear to have the most universal unlimited tendency
to the greatest and most extensive happiness of all the rational
agents to whom our influence can reach".[1] But Hutcheson, like

[1] Francis Hutcheson, *Inquiry Concerning Moral Good and Evil*, sect. iii, apud
L. A. Selby-Bigge, *British Moralists*, Oxford, 1897, vol. i, p. 108.

Shaftesbury, weakens his case by talking of the moral sense as if it were a kind of feeling. Really it is reason or intellect which enables us to acknowledge others as others and to recognize what is due to them. This older tradition of intellectualism is upheld in the eighteenth century by Samuel Clarke, John Balguy, and with special vigour by Richard Price.

Hutcheson's principle of the greatest happiness of the greatest number was taken over, of course, by Bentham and the utilitarians. Bentham sounds at the beginning of his *Introduction to the Principles of Morals and Legislation* as if he is going to proclaim an egoistic hedonism in the manner of Hobbes, but it soon becomes clear that he expects men in community to promote the happiness of the community even in preference to their private satisfaction. "A man may be said to be a partisan of the principle of utility", he says, "when the approbation or disapprobation he annexes to any action, or to any measure, is determined by and proportioned to the tendency which he conceives it to have to augment or to diminish the happiness of the community."[1] Where Bentham fails as a writer on social ethics is rather in his unimaginative account of happiness and of the uniform and measurable nature of pleasures and pains.

It is, indeed, obvious enough that in contrast with the limitations of self-interest the principles of right action must be of universal validity and tend towards what is absolutely good or good on the whole. This finds familiar expression in two of Kant's formulations of the categorical imperative: "Act only on that maxim which you can at the same time will to become a universal law"; "Act as if the maxim of your action were to become through your will a universal law of nature." The complementary aspect appears in Aristotle's repeated reference to right action as being τοῦ καλοῦ ἕνεκα, for the sake of the noble or the absolutely good, as distinguishable from the expedient or enlightened self-interest and the pleasant or the

[1] Jeremy Bentham, *Introduction to the Principles of Morals and Legislation*, ch. i, § ix.

greatest attraction of the moment. These principles amount to the same, for we can approve as a universal law only what transcends the bias of individual desire. Needless to say, the agent has very much to take his own good into account, but it evokes a moral response in so far as it enters into the objective good which his act might attain and is not pursued merely under the aspect of self-interest or immediate pleasure.

III

The moral situation is, therefore, one in which there is a choice between mere pleasure or self-interest and what is good when all its relations are taken into account. Moral obligation is a response to the absolutely good. We might be inclined to go on with G. E. Moore to hold that our moral obligation is to produce the greatest amount of good possible in the circumstances.

> Our "duty", therefore, can only be defined as that action, which will cause more good to exist in the Universe than any possible alternative. And what is "right" or "morally permissible" only differs from this, as what will *not* cause *less* good than any possible alternative.[1]

This doctrine is, of course, quite independent of Moore's rather odd view of good as an indefinable quality. It should be added that Moore is fully aware of at least one of the difficulties involved in it. Since we are ignorant of the full consequences of any action, we can arrive only at probable judgments about our duty in any case. But almost any ethical theory has at some stage to point out that it is right in the sense of morally praiseworthy to do what is probably right in a fully objective sense. Hence Moore is justified in thinking that this difficulty does not dispose of his theory.

[1] G. E. Moore, *Principia Ethica*, Cambridge, 1903, § 89, p. 148.

Yet we have only to recall one of the more fruitful discussions of ethical questions in the fairly recent past to encounter Sir David Ross's more forcible objections to Moore's theory. While Ross was willing to concede that many obligations could be explained on Moore's principle, he named as outstanding exceptions the obligations of fidelity to promises made, gratitude for benefits received and reparation for injuries inflicted.[1] If you have promised to give someone five pounds, it would usually be thought that you are bound to fulfil your promise even though you later come across someone in greater need of it. So you are bound to return benefits to the benefactor and to make reparation to the injured person even though you might employ your resources in other directions in a way which would do more good. It might be suggested in defence of Moore's point of view that the effect of fulfilling such obligations on the general good of society is always sufficient to outweigh any disadvantages in the particular case. But this is not very convincing. Would we not regard ourselves as bound by these obligations even if this were not the case? And do we not regard ourselves as so bound even though we can hardly be sure that it is the case? Moreover, if it were clearly true that we ought always to produce the greatest possible amount of good, how would it minister to the good of society to make what would then appear to be pedantic exceptions to the rule?

It might be added that, whenever we want to apply the rather vague adage that the end does not justify the means, meaning that a good end does not justify bad means, we are asserting that there are cases in which it is our duty to produce less than the greatest possible amount of good. For, if it were always right to produce the greatest possible amount of good, a greater positive value in the end would always justify bringing about a lesser disvalue as means. It would, for example, be permissible to assassinate a statesman who is leading the country into a destructive war. It would be permissible to rob the relatively

[1] Cf. W. D. Ross, *The Right and the Good*, Oxford, 1930, pp. 27, 34-9.

52

rich in order to assist the relatively poor. But we do not usually suppose that such acts are consonant with morality.

Finally, there is a still more fundamental objection to Moore's theory. This is that it imposes in every case an obligation of perfection. But we are accustomed to distinguish between what is strictly obligatory and what is more perfect. An intermediate class is usually allowed to exist between saints and sinners. To think otherwise would throw an intolerable burden on ordinary human nature. Yet the armchair moralist is somewhat prone to a theoretical perfectionism. Even so acute a thinker as Richard Price is evidently unhappy with the suggestion of derogating from it. He points out quite correctly that

> ... though the idea of rightness may be more general than that of fitness, duty, or obligation; so that there may be instances to which we apply the one, but not the other; yet this cannot be said of wrong. The idea of this, and of obligation, are certainly of the same extent; I mean, that though there may be cases in which it cannot be said, that what we approve as right, ought to have been done; yet there are no cases in which it cannot be said, that what is wrong to be done, or omitted, ought not to be done or omitted.[1]

Unfortunately, however, he goes back on this by suggesting that what appears to be non-obligatory rightness is merely the result of uncertainty about the extent of obligation and that whatever is definitely judged to be best is also obligatory.

This is surely too hard, but it is not easy to see on a scale of goodness, such as Moore offers, where exactly the line is to be drawn between the strictly obligatory and what goes beyond it. It would seem necessary to look more closely at the notion of goodness or value. Then we may be able to see both where strict obligation ends and why it is sometimes obligatory to aim at a lesser rather than a greater good.

[1] Richard Price, *Review of the Principal Questions in Morals*, ch. vi, apud Selby-Bigge, *British Moralists*, vol. ii, p. 167.

IV

The primary conceptions of good and evil which we need are correlative with the notion of substance. A substance is a nature, a unit of acting and being acted upon, a subject of potentialities which may be fulfilled variously and in different measure. Its good means the harmonious positive fulfilment of its potentialities; its evil lies in disharmony and frustration. As the notions of substance and nature are those first clearly presented by Aristotle, so also this conception of good is put forward with reference to man in his description of *eudaimonia* or happiness. It is commended here as a recognizably true interpretation of our ordinary ways of thinking and as turning out to give an acceptable meaning to our moral notions.

We have spoken of harmony and fulfilment, as of disharmony and frustration. Really it would be enough to speak of fulfilment and frustration alone. But the other terms remind us that with a multitude of possibly conflicting potentialities it is not the maximum development of any one but the harmonious development of all in their proportion which constitutes the maximum fulfilment of the whole. The professional athlete often finds to his cost in later life that the overdevelopment of his physical powers in one direction has had the reverse of a beneficial effect on his health as a whole. Something similar may be observed in the sphere of mind, as indeed also in the relations between body and mind. Specialization must not be overdone.

Another phrase to which we must recur is that things have to be thought of as units of acting and being acted upon. They are not in a static equilibrium. At any moment there is a next stage of development which is natural to them. Their good, therefore, consists not only in the preservation of what they have so far attained but in the fulfilment of their present natural tendency, and evil is not only what diminishes their achievement but what frustrates their natural development.

Our actions affect ourselves and others for good and for evil.

In a situation of free choice the good and the evil which we might bring about are presented to us. There we have that distinctive recognition that we *ought* to do good and to avoid evil. More precisely, we see that we ought to avoid evil and to do that good whose omission would be evil. The greater good makes a moral claim on us which is not strictly an obligation; the limits of strict obligation are to be determined under the negative aspect of the avoidance of evil. Needless to say, a great deal of positive activity may be needed in order simply to avoid evil, as in helping to rescue a drowning man, but conceptually the difference between obligation and perfection is between the avoidance of evil and the performance of greater good. This distinction seems to make clear the deliverances of moral instinct and to be essential to an adequate moral theory.

Thus we see that it is often necessary to forego immediate pleasure for the sake of our permanent fulfilment or to sacrifice our own pleasure or interest for the sake of what is due to others. The moral view of a situation is that which takes into account all the possible good and evil to be brought about according to our power of choice, not only for ourselves and still less for ourselves at that particular moment. Justice in its fullest sense sums up our duty towards others and implies that equality with which we should regard their interests in so far as they may be affected by our actions. But plenty of actions are wholly or mainly self-regarding. They come equally within the moral sphere in so far as there may be conflict between immediate impulse and permanent good.

To what other than ourselves do we owe duties? We cannot be said to owe duties to inanimate objects, for these are not susceptible of different degrees of fulfilment. Of any organism we might say in the abstract that we should use it in accordance with its nature, but it is difficult to see that this maxim could have any application to what is not at least sentient. That we have a duty of kindness in relation to animals is evident enough, for they can enjoy and suffer, but this has to be understood in a sense

55

compatible with the use of them for our purposes in accordance with their nature. We do not speak of duties to animals and rights of animals, for rights and duties in the proper sense are thought of as correlative and reciprocal, whereas animals, not being reflective and moral agents, can claim no rights and have no duties. Rights and duties in the proper sense exist in the relations of persons.

The religious man, however, holds that he has duties to God which are certainly no less binding than his duties to his neighbour. How does this fit with our analysis? The fulfilment of duty to God confers no benefit on the Creator. We must plainly admit that the only person benefited by it is the man who fulfils it. Should we then regard the duties of religion as self-regarding duties? That would sound extremely odd. The difficulty is resolved only when we see that we owe love to God, and with love the difference between self and other becomes irrelevant. But this requires more ample consideration to be appreciated. Hence we shall pursue the plan of dealing with ethics on the purely human level and leave to the end the transition from mere morality to religion.

So far we have discussed the situations in which moral claims arise, whether of strict obligation or of greater good. But we have not yet given a satisfactory account of moral judgment, for moral judgment has to consider the whole of the situation in which we find ourselves, and this is often of considerable complexity. If we are to know our duty, we must be able to reconcile conflicting moral claims. Problems of this kind demand treatment at some length.

Chapter VI

MORAL JUDGMENT

I

MORAL philosophers have often shown a curious disdain for casuistry. They have been reluctant to step down from the summits of airy abstraction to offer any help to the man who wants to know how to discover his duty in a concrete situation. This is rather like developing an elaborate theory of vitamins while declining to tell the cook in what foods they are to be found. No doubt we cannot expect the same clearness and certainty in particular moral conclusions that we might hope to find in general moral principles. Nevertheless the moral philosopher is scarcely doing his job unless he discusses how we may arrive at particular moral judgments.

Conscience is sometimes held to be a quasi-divine voice within us, but conscience is simply our capacity of moral judgment, and it is certainly not less fallible in its instinctive than in its reflective form. We are right in paying attention to our moral instincts as to our instinctive judgments in other matters. Common sense precedes reflection in every department of human thought, and reflection needs to keep common sense in mind lest it take too partial a view, overlooking part of what instinct has grasped vaguely and globally. But adequate reflection can improve on instinct not less in ethics than in other fields. There would be little point in arriving at general moral principles of a philosophical sort if we were left to instinct for our moral conclusions.

Sometimes, of course, the situation is simple enough. There is one clear duty to be done, and the only difficulty is in doing it.

But there are plenty of cases in quite ordinary life, and not merely in the ingenious constructions of moral casuists, where the plain man is faced by conflicting moral claims. Sir David Ross among moral philosophers has the merit of showing a proper awareness that the question needs attention. Something is my *prima facie* duty because, for example, it is the keeping of a promise, but I can foresee serious harm to someone which would result from my doing this. From the point of view of beneficence something else is my *prima facie* duty, but it involves breaking the promise. How am I to decide between these *prima facie* duties which is my duty proper? Unfortunately Ross has not much help to offer us in finding an answer.

> For the estimation of the comparative stringency of these *prima facie* obligations no general rules can, so far as I can see, be laid down.[1]

Just as Aristotle says about hitting the mean that the decision lies with a judgment which is like perception, so Ross tells us that we must weigh the factors for ourselves in each case and trust our final impression. If we want to see whether it is possible to go any farther, we must examine the maxims employed by moral casuists in settling their perplexities.

II

Human choices, like stones thrown in the water, produce far-reaching but gradually diminishing effects. Evidently the moral character of a choice depends not only on what is immediately brought about but on its ulterior effects in so far as these can reasonably be foreseen. The main purpose or motive entertained by the agent is of special importance for the moral qualification of his act, but he is not entitled to leave out of account any other consequences which he is able to expect. Hence possible choices

[1] W. D. Ross, *The Right and the Good*, p. 41. Cf. the whole of Chapter II.

which seem right from one point of view and wrong from another are by no means uncommon.

The plain man is likely to recognize the kind of conflict intended when he thinks of the old question, does the end justify the means? We are safe with a good end and good means, and there is no ambiguity about a bad end and bad means, nor is it difficult to see that what might be a good act is stultified when it is done as means to a bad end. To give money to a poor man is in general good, but not if it is the price of his doing a murder for you. But the question of attaining a good end by means which seem bad or would otherwise certainly be bad is not so easy.

To say that a good end cannot justify bad means may, of course, be a mere tautology if by "bad means" you intend precisely such as cannot cease to be bad or be justified by the purpose for which they are employed. But some maxims used in casuistry seem to imply that *prima facie* evil means can never be justified by any end. The principle of double effect states that an act with an evil effect is permissible only if a good effect is equally immediate and the situation as a whole justifies allowing the former for the sake of the latter. This seems to rule out any case in which the *prima facie* evil leads to the good intended, for the good is not then equally immediate.

The principle of double effect applies satisfactorily to a considerable number of cases. It is wrong to kill a man in order to relieve him from pain, but it is right to give him what will relieve his pain even though it may also tend to shorten life. This may be regarded as a controversial instance at a time when some favour euthanasia, but the distinction is one which the majority of men will still acknowledge as reasonable. Again, it is wrong for an occupying power to execute innocent hostages in order to deter saboteurs whom it is unable to detect, but it is right to warn someone against making an unsuitable marriage even though the reputation of the third person will be harmed. The principle also applies admirably to cases of co-operation or of assisting another person in doing wrong. A cab-driver would not be allowed to exercise his business if he wanted to pick and choose his passengers and their destinations. Hence he is morally justified in performing the intrinsically innocent action of driving a passenger from one point to another although he is aware that the destination is a house of ill fame. But he is under no such obligation, and it would be wrong for him, to select an address of the kind at the request of a stranger in the city.

There are other cases, however, in which we feel constrained to apply an opposite principle. If a man is after me with a revolver, I am justified in shooting him first in order to save my life. If there is no other way of protecting a legitimate secret, I may tell an untruth in order to prevent its diffusion. In such cases I seem to be doing what has hitherto been condemned, which is to take *prima facie* evil means in order to attain a rightful end.

The moralists usually bring such cases under the principle of the unjust aggressor. The would-be assassin is thought of as having lost his right to have his own life respected, and the man who seeks what it is not his business to know is thought of as having lost his right to a truthful answer. This is reasonable enough, but it hardly suffices to make a clear theoretical distinction from the cases in which I may not do evil in order that good may come. For the taking of life and the giving of false information remain in their different ways *prima facie* evils, and what justifies them in particular cases is precisely that they are unavoidable means to ends whose rightfulness is regarded as predominant. Does the fault of the aggressor constitute an essential difference? No, because his fault is precisely to oppose me in pursuing a rightful end, and, unless that end is taken into account, the *prima facie* badness of my act remains uncompensated.

Let us reflect again. What sort of case are we generally thinking about when we say that we may not do evil in order that good may come? The typical case is surely that in which we are considering whether we may neglect an obligation in order to achieve a greater good. If in a war we can deter the other side from shooting prisoners by threatening to shoot the prisoners whom we have taken, the temptation is obviously very great. It is in such a case that we have to remind ourselves that we have a strict moral obligation to respect the lives of our prisoners, and that obligation is affected neither by our opponents neglecting their similar obligations nor by the possibility of our attaining what we regard as a greater good by ourselves threatening to neglect it.

When some actions are regarded as permissible on the principle of double effect, the emphasis is on the factor of permissibility. We are not so much trying positively to determine our duty as to show that in a particular case there may be a factor which entitles us to neglect what would otherwise be our duty. This cannot merely be a greater good; it must be a strict right, to which a duty on the part of others corresponds. There are cases in which the assertion of a strict right entitles us to permit ulterior consequences which are *prima facie* evil.

This does not differ so much from the principle of the unjust aggressor, except that in the latter case the emphasis is on the duty of another rather than on my corresponding right. Consideration of the moral results of the neglect of duty by another may lead to cases in which my neglect of *prima facie* duty towards him is not only permissible but even obligatory. I may, for example, be not only permitted but actually bound to try to mislead someone who is seeking means to do an injury to another. These reflections may have cleared the ground sufficiently for an attempt to arrive at greater theoretical clearness about the principles by which the apparent conflict of duties is to be resolved.

III

We must begin by laying down more complex but clearer categories of thought. It is not enough to talk only of good and bad acts and consequences. We must distinguish duties and the rights corresponding to these on the part of another from greater goods which are not of obligation; this was discussed in the previous chapter. We must also distinguish ostensible or *prima facie* duties and rights from our final duties and rights or duties and rights proper. The former arise from partial and abstract considerations; the latter depend on all the factors of the case in its concreteness. We want to be able to determine our final duties and rights in different types of conflict between ostensible duties, ostensible rights and greater goods. When these distinctions are made, the relative immediacy of the effect does not seem to be significant if it is equally certain.

In a conflict between an ostensible duty and a greater good it is clear that we must prefer the ostensible duty, for this is the only source of obligation in the situation. The ostensible duty is our final duty. This includes the sort of case in which we are accustomed to say that the end does not justify the means.

In a conflict between an ostensible right and a greater good we are entitled to prefer the ostensible right. We are not bound to sacrifice what is due to us for the sake of a beneficence which is not of obligation, however praiseworthy it might be to do so.

In a conflict between ostensible duties we have to decide, if possible, which is the predominant duty. We need not suppose that this is always possible. If it is impossible, our choice is morally free. This type of case is obviously a chief source of moral perplexity. It is easy to see, in spite of the legal rigorism of such as Kant, that it is more important to save a life than to tell the truth if I can enable the intended victim to escape by misleading the assassin. But in less dramatic but more common cases it is not easy to see, for example, whether I ought to give someone good advice at the risk of hurting his feelings or to spare his feelings by leaving him without the advice he needs.

In a conflict between an ostensible right and an ostensible duty we have also to try to decide which is predominant, and this may again be difficult. Can I make sure of saving myself from some misfortune by leaving someone else in the lurch? The question is not whether this is the highest heroism but whether in a particular case it is morally permissible. We must at least be sure that we are not exposing another to greater evil than the evil from which we are saving ourselves, for we must certainly be content sometimes to forgo an ostensible right in order to fulfil a greater obligation. We cannot insist on the payment of a debt at a time when it would leave a man and his family to starve. The clearest cases of this sort are those which come under the classical formula of the unjust aggressor; the principle of double effect was devised mainly in order to deal with less clear cases of the same general type of a conflict between ostensible right and ostensible duty. Both these maxims, however, are applicable also to cases of conflict between ostensible duties, and their ambiguities arise from inattention to the distinction between goods which are ostensibly obligatory and goods which are not ostensibly obligatory.

A few more general remarks are necessary to round off the discussion. Since the effects of our actions stretch out into an indefinite future, it may be objected that we know so little about them that we must always be in a state of moral perplexity and can never make up our minds what we ought to do. It can surely be answered quite briefly that the nearer effects, of which we have some knowledge, are the more intense, and for the rest we can rely on the general probability that good will lead to good rather than evil. Hence we usually have sufficient grounds to make up our minds with that degree of probability which, in Butler's classical adage, is the guide to life.

Nevertheless we are sometimes left in perplexity with conflicting probabilities in favour of different courses of action. The point of the moral system called probabilism is that in such cases we are entitled to take any course which is probably right. Probabilism does not mean that it is morally permissible to do anything, however absurd, for which it is possible to advance any argument, however bad. It means that, when one alternative is not so clearly the more probably right that the other cannot be called probably right at all in any practical sense, we are morally free to choose between them. This is evidently reasonable, for in such a case there is no adequate foundation for an absolute obligation on either side. It should be emphasized, of course, that the probabilities are probable rights or duties, for probable facts are often the source of absolute obligations. We could not excuse a man who made no attempt to provide for his family in the event of his death on the ground that there was a genuine chance that he would survive them.

Finally, after doing our best to arrive at the right answer about what we ought to do, we may be mistaken. It remains true, unless we despair of human thought altogether, that, if we have done our best to think the matter out to the extent required, we are more likely to be right than wrong. Hence it is certainly right in a derivative sense to do what we think to be right in a primary sense. Or we can, if we like, distinguish a morally good action from an objectively right action. To do what we think to be right is always morally good even if it is not objectively right.

The discussion of moral perplexity is liable to give the impression that we cannot usually decide what we ought to do without an immense amount of hair-splitting. This is erroneous. Fortunately the most common cases are those in which we are able to see our duty with sufficient clearness after brief reflection or even without any special intellectual effort.

Chapter VII

MORALS AND INTELLIGENCE

I

THE heading of one of the chapters in Bernard Bosanquet's *Some Suggestions in Ethics* is: "We are not hard enough on stupidity." There is much to be said in favour of this statement. It seems to be commonly assumed by the plain man that moral instinct without reflection is sufficient to decide how to act rightly, that it is morally indifferent whether one uses one's brains or not, and even that the development of intelligence is injurious to the universal kindliness which the plain man tends to equate with the moral ideal. None of these opinions is evidently true. Indeed, the first two are fairly clearly false, and of the third it may be said that a certain discrimination in the exercise of kindliness is to be commended.

For the classical discussion of this subject we look back to the Platonic dialogues in which the question at issue is the identity of virtue and knowledge. At no time, of course, did Plato think that virtue was a subject to be taught like other subjects, a particular science like mathematics or a particular art like seamanship. The mistake of the sophists was to claim that they could teach men the science or art of citizenship. In the *Gorgias* Plato brings out at great length against the sophist of that name that what he is really teaching is rhetoric, the art of persuasion, an art which can be used for good or for ill. In so far as the well-trained orator can use his talents to influence his fellow-citizens in the public assembly, he can attain power and can make life pleasant for himself, but these things are not the final good or the ultimate source of happiness.

Against Protagoras, in the dialogue named after him, the Platonic Socrates emphasizes that virtues are not a collection of qualities which can be acquired one by one and can maintain themselves in isolation. It is absurd to think that a man can be genuinely virtuous in one respect and thoroughly vicious in another. While our natural advantages, even in the moral order, are different, an advance in virtue is an advance in the right use of all our tendencies. The sense in which virtue is one is more important than the sense in which we speak of many virtues.

So far it would seem that virtue, as we have come to understand it, has no teachers. But, if it could be taught, this would be so desirable that the absence of teachers would lead us to suppose that it cannot be taught and has nothing to do with knowledge. It is a kind of harmony in the soul, says Plato in the *Gorgias*, a state in which desires are tempered in order and proportion.

But then, as Plato points out in the *Meno*, what is needed in order to guide and govern human tendencies aright is wisdom. Without wisdom even the most brilliant qualities can go astray; the possession of wisdom is the necessary condition of their right use. Virtue, therefore, is founded in wisdom, and wisdom, as an intellectual quality, ought to be teachable. If there are as yet no teachers of virtue, and even the best men usually hold their moral principles rather as a matter of sound instinctive opinion than as a matter of systematic knowledge, this shows only that there is a vast gap to be filled. If our civic affairs so often go awry, it is because we have not yet discovered how to communicate that wisdom which is the foundation of virtue.

The picture, in the *Republic*, of the wise and virtuous man as one who has contemplated, and keeps his mind fixed on, the form of the Good, makes clearer the kind of unity of virtue and knowledge which Plato wants to inculcate. Knowledge of the forms is a knowledge of ideal standards. Plato was convinced that we fully exercise the power of intellectual judgment only when we relate mere facts to standards of completeness and perfection. All forms or standards of judgment participate, because they are standards, in goodness or perfection. The form of the Good is the supreme form because it is the standard of standards. When we not only evaluate things by standards but evaluate the standards themselves by relation to the standard of standards, our knowledge can be properly described as wisdom.

When Plato reached this point, he saw that, even if virtue could be described in terms of knowledge, the knowledge which was wisdom could not be communicated in the same way as any other kind of knowledge. Wisdom, being a grasp of the standard of standards, the form of the Good, might be described, in all seriousness and without any suggestion of triviality, as the apotheosis of good taste. This sublimation of good taste could not be the object of formal teaching; it had to come in a flash, but as the consummation of effort and of communication with minds already practised in it. This is the burden of the passage in the *Seventh Letter*, in which Plato explained why he could never write a treatise on the subject and still more deprecates the attempt of anyone else to do so. Plato knew how to draw the bounds of what could be said.

The clearest lesson to be drawn from Plato's discussion is the futility of trying to divorce morals and intelligence. Although the primary subject of moral qualifications is the self freely choosing, a man cannot know how to choose rightly unless he applies his intelligence, and his intelligence itself is misdirected and unfulfilled if he does not seek to act rightly. In considering intellectual duties more analytically we must not lose sight of the due unity of thought and action upon which their value depends.

II

The term which in Plato is best rendered in a wider sense as wisdom (φρόνησις) may be translated in Aristotle as "prudence". But this is not prudence in the narrow modern sense of avoiding risks; it is the capacity of judging accurately what is right or wrong. This capacity, as Aristotle correctly points out, goes hand in hand with moral virtue, the habit of right action, for the man who is going to act wrongly seeks as far as possible to avoid facing the fact that what he is doing is wrong, while the man who wants to act rightly tries to see as clearly as possible what really is right.

The medieval philosophers used the odd derivative *synderesis* (from συντήρησις) for the power of moral judgment; *conscientia* applied to its actual exercise. Prudence was, then, in its Aristotelian sense, a habit of the mind under the aspect of *synderesis*, and St. Thomas Aquinas is as insistent as any Greek on the necessity of cultivating an intelligent discrimination of right and wrong. The playing down of the proper part of thought in morality is a modern aberration quite uncharacteristic of the high Middle Ages.

There is also a fundamental moral virtue in the conduct of thought, which is sincerity or integrity of mind. It is the valuable element in what the contemporary existentialist calls "authenticity", being yourself, although this term is occasionally perverted to justify oddity for its own sake. It is important to note that this is not merely a virtue of the intellectual. Every man, whatever his intellectual capacity may be, is capable of thinking honestly according to his lights and of expressing his opinion sincerely. He can take whatever means are at his disposal for distinguishing truth from falsehood and can refrain from assertion on what he knows nothing about. The importance of avoiding any hurt to intellectual honesty and sincerity is the principal motive for tolerance of opinions and their expression, even when the opinions are judged to be dangerously mistaken. Can it be said that the plain man today is sufficiently aware of what is involved in intellectual integrity? Many a man who would not dream of telling a lie seems to care little on what his opinions are based and will take no trouble to correct them.

It is rather a harder saying when the highest form of human life is said to be the intellectual life, as Aristotle maintains with vigour in the latter half of the tenth book of the *Nicomachean Ethics*. We can indeed argue in the abstract that thinking is the noblest function of man and that, consequently, a life devoted to thought is the finest kind of life, but it is almost unduly evident that only a minority of men are fitted for it. Aristotle, after all, was thinking of a select minority of leisured property-owners, not of mankind in general. What can be said, not only without absurdity but with very much relevance, is that it is just as much a duty to develop whatever intellectual powers a man has as to develop his powers of action. Since intellectual development is by no means the luxury that it is sometimes alleged to be but involves a good deal of hard work, this duty is at least as likely to be neglected as any other. The moral philosopher should not, therefore, omit to call attention to it.

It is foolish, then, to try to divorce morals and intelligence. The man who cultivates his brains for wrong or inadequate ends deserves no more than the semi-pejorative epithet of "clever", and the man whose attempts to act rightly are guided by mere sentiment can only be dismissed as well-meaning. Wisdom in the Platonic sense is the prerogative, in some measure at least, of all who make the best use of all their powers.

Chapter VIII

MORAL CHARACTER

I

ONE of the merits of Aristotelian ethics is that Aristotle treats of morality not only in terms of right acts, but with regard to habits of right action and their integration in a fully developed human character. Although men evidently differ in their innate qualities, so that the generic potentialities of human nature are already determined in some measure by heredity, their characters begin with a relatively high degree of plasticity. But acts tend to form habits. Hence, as we observe, men gradually become more determinate in their modes of action as life goes on. In Aristotelian terms, the range of potentialities which was their original substantial nature has been modified by habitual dispositions which incline them to act in the same way when similar circumstances recur.

Such habits may be ethically indifferent, like the capacity to speak French or do carpentry or drive a car. But a habit of right action is what Aristotle means by a moral virtue, and a habit of wrong action is a vice. Virtues and vices have, therefore, to be seen in relation to the original impulses or instincts to which they give a specific direction and in relation to the whole character which they contribute to build.

Later Greek philosophy evolved a scheme of the original impulses or passions, due, it would seem, to Posidonius, but based on the image of the soul offered by Plato in the fourth book of the *Republic*. The three levels of the soul in its activity are there said to be the basic element of desire, the spirited or combative part, and the reason, whose function it is to govern the other two. The passions, in the scheme inherited by the Middle Ages from Hellenistic philosophy, are divided between the desirous or concupiscent element and the spirited or irascible element. We are reminded of Freud's distinction between the instincts of libido in its generalized sense and the instincts of aggression, life-instincts and death-instincts, a distinction which is fundamentally Platonic.

To the concupiscent appetite belong love and hate as directed towards good and evil in general, joy and sadness as directed towards present good and evil, and desire and aversion as directed towards future good and evil. To the irascible appetite belong hope and despair, as good is thought to be easy or difficult to attain, boldness and fear, as evil is thought to be easy or difficult to avoid, and anger as directed towards the removal of evil. Similar classifications continued to be a feature of moral philosophy down to Descartes and to Hume.

The virtues, then, might be specified as the habits of rightly controlling these fundamental attitudes towards good and evil in general, or they might be specified as governing our attitudes towards the different kinds of good and evil which we naturally desire. Ordinary language, as we might expect, has not tidily adopted either point of view to the exclusion of the other. The disentanglement of the various and sometimes conflicting shades of meaning in the terms used to designate virtues and vices is an appropriate field for linguistic analysis of a more detailed kind than demands to be undertaken here.

If, however, we think of virtue as achieving a due proportion and harmony between our natural desires, the fundamental virtue of individual ethics is, in a term whose associations have become ridiculously restricted in modern times, the virtue of temperance. Temperance, in the Greek sense, is precisely the habit of so moderating the force of specific desires that they co-operate in an activity which fulfils the nature of man as a whole. That fulfilment is the Aristotelian εὐδαιμονία, the full activity of man in accordance with right principle, a maximum development of the whole which results from an optimum exercise of the partial tendencies. Since virtue requires also a due development of the combative spirit in opposition to difficulty, we may speak also of a fundamental virtue of courage or fortitude. If we add that virtue presupposes the sound judgment which belongs to wisdom or prudence and that the general name for virtue in relation to others is justice, we have completed the traditional list of the cardinal virtues, which run through Greek and medieval moral thinking with an occasional variation of meaning but a persistent maintenance of label.

It is in so far as virtue has the aspect of temperance that it most clearly verifies the Aristotelian doctrine of the mean. The maximum fulfilment of man as a whole, we may repeat, involves proportion and harmony among his specific tendencies. The right development of each is not a maximum but a mean which contributes to the proper proportion of the whole. Hence the interplay of positive and negative among accepted moral precepts. The important point is that the negative is always in the end for the sake of the positive. A merely negative morality, self-denial for the sake of self-denial, has lost the only possible justification of moral restraint, its contribution to the positive fulfilment of human nature as a whole. To take a crucial example, the very strength of the sexual instinct calls for such resolute measures of control that it is easy for the too negatively-minded moral man to forget that all such measures are intended to canalize it for the purpose for which it really fulfils man as a social being. In the life of the family, in the mutual relations of father, mother and children, the sexual instinct is the source of some among the greatest of moral values. So it is with all our instincts, that they are to be negatively controlled for the sake of achieving their greatest positive value in the whole context of human life.

The development of moral character consists, then, in the formation of habits of right action, the virtues, which contribute in harmony and proportion to the fulfilment of human nature as a whole. In so far as men are alike, the same moral precepts apply to all. In so far as they differ, each has a different calling, a different mode of development in detail, a different place in the world of men. Each in his different way has to use his freedom of choice in order to reach that freedom from evil, that stability in the right, which makes him not merely a doer of isolated right actions but a good man.

II

In the absence of the right moral development which we have sketched as far as is necessary on account of the fairly obvious nature of the matter, there may be the opposite extreme of the fully deliberate adoption of wrong ends, the cynically avowed preference for pleasure or self-interest when these conflict with what is right. What is more common, however, is probably the habit of taking the line of least resistance and yielding to the most urgent impulse of the moment. While the pursuit of self-interest, since it often conflicts with immediate pleasure, involves calculation and self-control, the surrender to immediate pleasure need involve no more than the neglect of adequate thought and effort. This weakness of will is analysed by Aristotle in the seventh book of the *Ethics* in some of his psychologically acutest writing.

While the profligate and the weakling often act in the same way, they differ because the profligate chooses pleasure for its own sake with all his heart and the weakling chooses it because he has no will to resist. Unrestraint, as opposed to self-discipline, in relation to pleasure, is distinguished by Aristotle from softness, as opposed to endurance, in relation to pain. Since the two defects usually go together, this distinction is not of great importance, but Aristotle makes a more significant distinction between the sources of moral defect. In one sort of case it is the overwhelming strength of immediate impulse which carries all before

73

it; in the other sort of case the will is too weak to make a prolonged resistance to the continued assault of evil inclination.

From all this it is apparent in what moral education consists. The man who wants to be able to form right habits must first learn not to be carried away on the spur of the moment but to give himself time to consider what he is doing. He must learn also to persist in the effort to choose rightly even when it involves a prolonged struggle with inclination. And all this is for the sake of attaining not a stoic indifference to pleasure or prosperity but a consistent form of the good life in which rightful pleasure and genuine self-interest have their proper place. To enlarge upon these reflections belongs to the province of the preacher rather than of the moral philosopher, but the way in which they are related to philosophical principles deserves to be noticed.

Chapter IX

LAW AND MORALITY

I

AN OLD and respectable tradition refers to the law of states as positive law in distinction from the natural law of morality. Since Bentham and Austin, English thinkers have been wary of this distinction. The only clear notion of law is said to be that of laws which actually exist in the statute book or equivalently, and which are actually enforced. No doubt there is an ideal of law, to which actual laws only imperfectly approximate, but it is misleading to describe this as if it were actually law.

The controversy about natural law might by some be considered as merely verbal. It is generally admitted that there is morality as well as law, and that the legislator ought to take morality into account. Does it matter, then, whether we call morality a natural law or not? It matters, we may answer, to the extent that the difference of terminology tends to correspond with a difference about what we consider to be central and most important in the notion of law. Hence the controversy is not purely verbal, but our discussion may equally well at the beginning be described in neutral terms as being about the relationship of law and morality.

Laws, as we commonly know them, are general rules laid down by the supreme authority in the State under a penal sanction. We might want so to emphasize the importance of the sanction as to make laws into hypothetical imperatives. "If you do not want to be hanged, do not commit murder—either do not commit murder or be hanged." "If you do not want to be fined, do not exceed the speed limit—either observe the speed limit or pay a fine." On such an interpretation there would be a strong contrast between the hypothetical imperative of law and the categorical imperative of morality, for, however much we look to divine justice to provide morality itself with a sanction, this is incidental to the moral imperative. The moral imperative is essentially absolute or categorical.

But such an interpretation of law is plainly erroneous. The legislator is not indifferent whether the citizens commit murder or incur hanging, observe the speed limit or pay a fine. The law is first a command to do what is deemed to be right in the circumstances and the sanction is a secondary consideration intended to enforce the command where good will is absent. On his part the free and reasonable citizen will obey a sound law because he acknowledges its soundness and not merely in order to escape the consequences of disobedience. On this score, then, there is no essential contrast between law and morality, but the primary force of law is derived from the moral order.

It remains, however, that laws are universal rules to be applied equally in all instances. Even when provision is made for exceptions, these exceptions are themselves usually determined by a universal rule, so that in effect the law simply becomes a rather more elaborate universal rule. Provision for individual exceptions is frowned upon as opposed to the objective and impersonal character of law. Where the application of the law is doubtful, a court is justifiably interested in the merits of the particular case, but, where there is no such doubt, the court has to give a decision in accordance with the law even though it seems to be, or actually is, unfair. When such cases are frequent, it is for the legislature to rectify by a new and improved statute the injustice which was involved in the clumsy drafting of the statute which was previously in force.

The judgment about the morality of an act does, no doubt, involve weighing the universal aspects which it manifests, but the final judgment is a response to this individual case in its individuality. Every particular case has a certain uniqueness. To say something, for example, would be kind but it would not be truthful. When should we be kind at the expense of a certain economy of the truth while avoiding the lie direct? When is it better to be candid in spite of apparent unkindness? No general rules, however elaborate, will enable us to answer such questions. We have to try to cultivate a delicate response to the particular character of each case as it arises.

Here, then, is a more profound contrast between law and morality. We have to see whether it is so profound as to make it misleading to talk about morality in terms of law. In order to see this we must examine the moral foundation of human laws as we know them.

II

Men, living in society, have mutual rights and duties. They are liable both to disagree about what these are and to refuse to perform their obligations. If it were left to each man to enforce as best he could what he supposed to be his rights, human life, as Hobbes pithily pointed out, would be nasty, brutish and short. Hence it is necessary for the proper fulfilment of human nature that there should be a concentration of the power of coercion in the supreme authority of the State. No social contract need be supposed for the surrender or restriction of individual human rights in favour of the State; the necessity of the State is inherent in the human situation. The right of the State to obedience in general is due to the indispensable function which it fulfils.

But it would be agreed by most that it fulfils this function best by the application of a code of universal rules. This seems on reflection to be more paradoxical than its general acceptance would suggest. Plato makes us realize in the *Statesman* how paradoxical it is. A physician who applied exactly the same treatment to every instance of a type of disease without permitting himself any individual diagnosis or variation of remedy would scarcely be a candidate for Harley Street. In every art the best practitioner is the most sensitive to individual differences. Yet, except when doubt permits a certain latitude, we ask our judges for the most part to decide under what general rule a particular case comes and then to apply that rule to it without any greater latitude than is allowed in the rule itself. If their natural sympathies make them exceed this limit even to a minor degree, the appeal court has unkind remarks to make.

When men tire of the rigid rule of law, they set up what we nowadays call people's courts to consider each case on its own merits with a fine disregard for general principle. What could be better than to consider each case solely on its merits? Yet the results of doing so are somewhat disconcerting. So also, when men have tired of constitutional government and have acclaimed a leader or dictator whose vision is not to be hampered by petty legal restrictions, it is with a sigh of relief that they return later, whenever they are able to do so, to the humdrum rule of law. Plato himself had had a hankering for the perfect ruler who would be superior to laws and constitutions, but the discussion in the *Statesman* marks his final abandonment of this theoretically attractive but practically disastrous ideal.

The chief reason for adherence to a system of general rules of law is to be found in the exceedingly complex character of social relations. Even in purely individual ethical problems we have often to be content to act on a probability. When the social relations of men are concerned and the possible repercussions do not stop short of the social structure as a whole, we have certainly to be content with probability about what will produce the right result. If we tried to form an entirely new probable judgment in every particular case, we should be more than likely to leave half the relevant factors out of account. By contrast, a system of general rules which have been gradually established and which are capable of gradual improvement and adaptation to changing circumstances is far more likely to be adequate to a highly complex type of situation and to produce what will more nearly be the right result in a majority of cases. For the sake of this it is worth while even to permit the law to weigh heavily on what are acknowledged to be hard cases as long as such cases can be regarded as exceptional.

The value of a system of law, therefore, depends on its being applied to a field of probability rather than of certain knowledge and to a field wherein the factors whose probability is to be assessed are more complex than are susceptible of full consideration in every individual case. The universal character of legal rules does not, then, separate law from morality. These rules, if they are justified at all, do not demand obedience in any fundamentally different way from the claims of simple moral obligation. We ought to obey them because and in so far as their maintenance tends on the whole and in the majority of cases to the proper fulfilment of men as social beings. If laws thus derive their binding force from morality, it is not misleading to speak of morality as possessing even more fundamentally the character of law, provided that we do not turn morality into a code of absolutely rigid rules and forget the exceptions inherent in individual moral judgment. For that is what is meant by the reproach of taking a legalistic view of ethics.

III

Having worked back from law to morality, we may look at the situation from the reverse point of view, proceeding from morality to law. Morality covers the whole field of right and wrong, individual and social, but, if we regard the primary feature of law as being its claim to unconditional obedience, morality as a whole is the fundamental law of nature. So, for St. Thomas Aquinas, natural law is "the participation of eternal law in a rational creature", the reflection in a finite mind of the objective and timelessly valid rules by which its activity should be governed.[1]

Traditional views about the extent of natural law have varied, however, according to the emphasis placed on the factor of human understanding. If only that is said to belong to natural law which is recognized by all men to be such, it tends to be reduced to the vanishing point of tautologies such as that right should be done and wrong avoided. The distinction between primary precepts of natural law, which every normal man acknowledges, and secondary precepts, about which error is possible, is intended to remedy this difficulty. Even so, there is always an ambiguity about terms whose meaning is partly subjective and partly objective. We are inclined either to safeguard the objectivity of natural law by exaggerating its degree of general recognition or to make such allowances for the vagaries of history that it ceases to stand for anything of importance. It is really clearer to distinguish simply between an ideal of morality and the extent to which it is acknowledged by men at any given time and place. The ethical thinker, in so far as he is a reformer, tries to point out aspects of the ideal which are overlooked by his contemporaries.

It is not the business of the individual as such to enforce right action on other men, but he is entitled to do so if their wrong-doing conflicts with his own rights. Or rather, as we have already mentioned, since the result would be anarchy if every individual were his own judge in such matters, the social character of man demands a social authority whose function it is to enforce justice in human society. The purpose of the State thus defines its proper function. While it should be concerned to provide the circumstances in which individual personality can fulfil itself, it does this by establishing order in social relations, and the proper field of application of its supreme power of coercion is the field of social relations, not that of individual personality.

[1] St. Thomas Aquinas, *Summa Theologica*, I[a], II[ae], qu. 91, art. ii, c.

A long time was needed before men saw this principle clearly, and the events of our own day have shown that its hold on their minds is still precarious. Hence it deserves a certain amount of elaboration. Totalitarianism in the full sense, which sets the State above morality, must evidently be rejected as contrary to the unconditional claims of ethics. Yet, even when the supremacy of morality is acknowledged, there remains a milder sort of totalitarianism, according to which the enforcement of every kind of right action is, theoretically at any rate, within the competence of the State. This paternalism is not quite so easily seen to be mistaken.

Not only is Plato's ideal *Republic* decisively paternalistic, but the same principle is upheld in the more moderate and practical project of the *Laws*.

> Should anyone think to set forth laws for States, determining what should be their proper course in common and public matters, but holds that there is no need to regulate private affairs, however fundamental, and that everyone has the right to pass the day just as he likes rather than having to do everything by rule, supposing that, if private affairs are left outside the law, common and public matters will be willingly pursued in accordance with the laws, he thinks wrongly.[1]

In the same way Aristotle insists on the essentially social character of man to such an extent that he declares the State to be "prior in nature" to families and to individuals and so to have an unrestricted predominance over them. The *Politics* look as if, had they been completed, they would have offered as minute and comprehensive a system of regulations for the life of the citizen as anything that Plato projected.

It was left for the Middle Ages and St. Thomas Aquinas to arrive at a principle of political liberty. In his treatment of law Aquinas proceeds gradually to define the field of competence of the law of the State. At first he justifies the fact that legislation

[1] Plato, *Laws* VI, 779 E – 780 A.

does not prohibit all kinds of vice on grounds of expediency rather than of principle, saying that, since such comprehensive laws could not be carried into effect among men as they are, their failure would encourage disobedience to those more modest laws which can be enforced. Hence the legislator must be content if he can repress the greater evils, but Aquinas pregnantly adds that the evils to be repressed by law are chiefly those which result in harm to persons other than the agent and tend to destroy the peace and order of society.[1] He goes on to say more definitely that, while there is no kind of good act which might not be commanded by law, an act can be thus commanded only when it is called for by the common good.[2] His final expression of principle is as follows:

> Human law is ordained for the sake of civil society, which is that of men in their mutual relations. But the mutual relations of men arise from the external acts by which men affect one another. Now this reciprocity of action belongs to the sphere of justice, which is the proper norm of human society. Therefore human law does not prescribe acts other than those of justice, or, if it prescribes acts of other virtues, it does this only in so far as they take on the character of justice.[3]

This Thomistic principle of liberty was far from commanding general acceptance. Half a century after Aquinas, Marsilius of Padua, consciously reverting to the doctrines of antiquity, assigned once again to the State an unrestricted power of regulation over the whole field of human activity. The Renaissance monarchies acted in the spirit of Marsilius. The most intelligent of the defenders of absolute monarchy, Thomas Hobbes, claimed that the necessity of the State for the preservation of mankind from a war of each against all gave rise to a duty of unquestioning obedience to the State in every case except when the action of

[1] St. Thomas Aquinas, *Summa Theologica*, Iᵃ IIᵃᵉ, qu. 96, art. ii.
[2] Aquinas, *Summa*, qu. 96, art. iii.
[3] Aquinas, *Summa*, qu. 100, art. ii.

the State threatened that preservation of life and order for the sake of which it existed.

Nevertheless, the principle of liberty was congenial to the spirit of English law, and, by what might seem to be a rather unlikely historical accident, Thomistic political theory was transmitted through Hooker to Locke and became not the least of England's contributions to the modern world. When we read John Stuart Mill *On Liberty*, we are reading one who in this department is an unconscious Thomist. His leading maxims are sufficiently well known.

> The maxims are, first, that the individual is not accountable to society for his actions, in so far as these concern the interests of no person but himself. Advice, instruction, persuasion, and avoidance by other people if thought necessary by them for their own good, are the only measures by which society can justifiably express its dislike or disapprobation of his conduct. Secondly, that for such actions as are prejudicial to the interests of others, the individual is accountable, and may be subjected either to social or to legal punishment, if society is of opinion that the one or the other is requisite for its protection.[1]

Mill has been criticized on the ground that his distinction cannot be upheld. There are no acts without social consequences. This seems somewhat like objecting to the distinction between blue and green because there are intermediate shades which are difficult to name. But, as with blue and green, there are sufficient actions whose significance is predominantly personal and sufficient actions whose significance is predominantly social to make the distinction applicable in a majority of cases. And such a distinction must be made. The individual is not answerable to society for his purely personal concerns. He is answerable to society for his actions in so far as these affect others, and that is in so far as they take on the character of justice or injustice.

[1] J. S. Mill, *On Liberty*, ch. v.

Our picture would, however, be incomplete without a reference to the Aristotelian distinction between distributive and corrective or commutative justice. Distributive justice is the justice of society towards its members in the fair apportionment of advantages and burdens. Commutative justice, presupposing distributive justice, is concerned with equality in exchange and the mutual observance of rights and duties among individuals. The State enforces duties of commutative justice, giving protection to life and limb, to property and to reputation, laying down conditions for valid contracts and ensuring the fulfilment of legal engagements. But, if such reciprocity in transactions is to be accepted as just, the fundamental distribution of privileges and burdens must be just, and each citizen must, as far as the circumstances of the time permit, have an adequate opportunity of self-development.

Difficulties in reconciling the claims of distributive and of commutative justice are the most important source of legitimate political differences. Ideally speaking, there ought to be agreement about what can strictly be called political philosophy. Both amoral totalitarianism and the milder paternalism can be rejected on clear general grounds of reason. But, given human fallibility and the fact that more specific questions have to be determined on grounds of probability, there will always be a tension between the conservative mind, insisting on commutative justice within the established order, and the progressive mind, with a livelier sense of need for greater fairness in distribution. Just as what was called *laissez-faire* liberalism involved a rather exclusive emphasis on commutative justice, so the contemporary reaction may well be accused of an exclusive emphasis in the other direction. But there is no hope of any general agreement with a detailed attempt to describe the happy mean. There we have passed beyond political philosophy into the realm of practical politics, and the best hope is that each side will be strong enough to exert a moderating influence on the other.

IV

Morality, then, as the source of the obligatory character of law, may itself be described as natural law. In a narrower sense we may mean by natural law that part of morality which it is the province of positive law to enforce, that is, the realm of justice or of social relationships. But morality itself demands that there should be certain social institutions without which human life could not attain its proper fulfilment. Such institutions are positive in so far as they have to be established by society, but natural in so far as they are demanded by morality. Hence, whatever we may hold to be morally demanded in the institutions, for example, of the family or of property, may be said to constitute another province and to define another meaning of natural law. It would be desirable to distinguish a good deal more clearly between these various meanings of natural law than is commonly done.

Beyond any limits within which ethical demands may be considered as clearly ascertainable, and with the need of change from time to time in order to meet changing circumstances, positive law has a freer field for the establishment of such social order and regulation as seems necessary for the proper fulfilment of human life at a particular time and at a particular place. Even so, positive law is not dissociated from the natural law of morality. Not only is it bad law if it is contrary to natural right and wrong, but it should always be based on a probable judgment about what is most fitting in the circumstances.

The mention of bad law must be slightly expanded. If the obligatory character of law is derived from morality, not only is a law contrary to morality not obligatory but opposition to it, when the occasion arises, is obligatory. Such a law is merely the outward husk of a law with the apparatus of physical enforcement belied by its ethical nullity. Human history would be considerably poorer without the record of conscientious objection to unjust laws.

But what of mistaken conscientious objection? Indeed, since

neither governments nor individual citizens can rightly claim infallibility, the practical problem is best considered in subjective terms as a clash of convictions. The maxim of the legal rigorist has always been that error as such has no rights, but there is an equally valid maxim that sincerity as such has rights. Hence, when there is a genuine conflict of moral view between a government and some of its subjects, the sincerity of the dissentients deserves to be respected, although the government has the right to test it by putting them in a position no better than is occupied by those who obey the law. When the conduct of dissentients might be prejudicial to the rest of the population, their liberty may have to be restrained, but this restraint cannot properly be given the stigma of punishment. It is part of the prudence of a legislator to try to avoid provoking such conflicts even in what seems to him to be a good cause, for general acceptability is one of the criteria of desirable legislation.

A more common case is that of legislation which can be regarded as trivial, pernickety or in any other way unnecessary. If a law does not conduce to the good of human society, even though it does not command anything intrinsically wrong, it cannot directly convey a moral obligation of obedience. It may, of course, be incumbent on the citizen to obey it in order not to spread a bad example of disobedience to law in general, and it is still clearer that an unnecessary law may be obeyed from the intelligible motive of avoiding fine or imprisonment. But the modern passion for detailed legislation affords plenty of examples in which no reasonable person regards disobedience as morally blameworthy. The multiplication of trivial regulations is especially to be avoided on the ground that it tends to bring law in general into contempt.

We should not omit the more edifying maxim that lawful authority should be given the benefit of the doubt where the doubt is serious. But it is equally incumbent on lawful authority to make itself intelligible and acceptable to its subjects. The importance of a convincing preamble to new legislation is not to be overlooked.

Chapter X

REWARD AND PUNISHMENT

I

THE consideration of law would be incomplete unless we looked at the moral basis of its sanctions, and what is true of punishment will presumably be applicable in a converse way to reward. Although there seem at first to be sharply opposed theories of punishment, the concessions which the proponents of each usually make to the others in the course of discussion make the difference notably less acute. Nevertheless, even differences of emphasis have their importance.

The plain man might begin by saying that there is no mystery about punishment. It is deserved; a guilty act demands to be punished. That is to say, we tend to assume prior to reflection what is described after reflection as the retributive theory of punishment. But it is not difficult to show the plain man that the matter is less clear than he might suppose. To inflict suffering on an offender seems merely to be adding the evil of suffering to the evil of the offence itself. To hang a murderer does not bring the murdered man back to life; what we are left with are two dead men.

Consequently we look for some other motive to supply the ground of punishment. We find the motive of deterrence, the effect which the contemplation of punishment has on those who might otherwise perpetrate the same sort of wrong act. Besides, we may hope to reform the criminal by punishment. This seems a much more positive and worthy aim than punishment for the sake of punishment, and any humane legislation must seek above all to reform wrongdoers. Hence we might want to say that retribution is a primitive notion belonging to the bad old days and that punishment must nowadays be conceived entirely in terms of deterrence and, especially, of reformation.

Yet guilt is at least a necessary condition of punishment. Deterrence might sometimes be achieved by penalizing the innocent, as when an occupying power shoots hostages to prevent attacks on its soldiers and officials. If a man, though innocent, were thought to be guilty, his punishment would have the same deterrent effect on others as if he had really been guilty. Such measures would be unjust precisely because they penalize the innocent. Hence we must take retribution into account, at least in the sense that guilt implies liability to punishment.

Moreover, a past wrong act is not only a necessary condition of the just infliction of punishment, but the extent of past guilt limits the extent of the punishment which it is right to inflict. Otherwise we should be justified in punishing more severely than others, in the interests of deterrence, precisely those wrong acts which men commit more easily because they regard them as comparatively trivial. A considerable good would be achieved if drivers observed the speed limits more exactly, but the public conscience would not at present tolerate the infliction of enormous penalties for excessive speed on a clear straight road. This is because they would seem disproportional to the guilt involved as the average man assesses it.

Reformation is in itself a benefit, not a punishment, and, if it can be brought about with the consent of the person concerned, it needs no further justification. But, if it involves restraint on him, it takes on the aspect of punishment as well. Could we approve of exercising restraint on the normal responsible adult for the sake of improving him unless he had made himself liable to it by doing wrong? The answer is evidently negative. Only when a man has incurred guilt can he be rightly subjected to force for the sake of reforming him.

Punishment cannot, therefore, be explained if we omit the

factor of retribution. Suitable purposes for inflicting punishment are, no doubt, reformation and deterrence, but guilt is a necessary presupposition. The question which we have to ask about the retributive factor is how it makes punishment justifiable or appropriate.

II

Retribution cannot, of course, be equated with compensation. If I have been the cause of your suffering loss, I can be legally compelled to make it up to you as far as is possible, but this is not punishment. The distinction between the fields of civil and of criminal proceedings is not always easy for the layman to appreciate, but there is a clear distinction of principle between a case where compensation is enough and a case in which punishment is demanded.

Compensation in a wider sense verges on the notion of punishment. A fine may sometimes be interpreted as a compensatory disadvantage inflicted by society on one who has enjoyed an unwarranted advantage from society. You have parked your car in a place in which parking is prohibited, and you pay for the stolen privilege.

But however much we stretch the notion of compensation, it will not cover the more notable cases of punishment. The hanging of the murderer does not in any way make up for the death of the victim, nor does a term in prison repair the crime for which it was inflicted. That is why a too simple theory of retribution, typified by the Hegelian assertion that punishment negates the wrong, is insufficient. For the majority of punishments just do not negate the wrong in any immediately intelligible sense.

Yet this over-simple doctrine is constantly repeated. Kant held it to be an evident moral principle that crime demands punishment, and a punishment equivalent in kind to the evil done.

Bradley says that a criminal is a standing assertion of wrong, and that the punishment is the annihilation of this wrong. Bosanquet thinks that a bad will is negated by the reaction of the social will for good. When compensation in any sense is possible, all this is true and to the point, but the most important forms of punishment cannot be reduced to compensation. They do not annihilate the wrong done.

How, then, should we interpret the factor of retribution? We must look for something deeper than a direct relation between the wrong act and its punishment, and must consider the lasting effects of wrongdoing in the deterioration of the character of the agent. A wrong act is the misuse of a power and tends to predispose towards its future misuse. This is what justifies the deprivation or restraint of powers which have been misused and are, consequently, likely to be misused again. A man has made himself liable to punishment by making himself such that he cannot, at least for a time, be trusted by society with the free use of his powers. Imprisonment implies a judgment that he can no longer be trusted with liberty, and capital punishment implies a judgment that he has so hopelessly misused his life that it is appropriate to put an end to it. Punishment becomes intelligible in its relation, not directly to the wrong act, but to the effects of the wrong act on the agent.

That a converse principle applies to the basis of reward is clear enough, and this justifies the appearance of reward in the title of this chapter, although discussion has, as is usual, turned on the more disturbing question of the ground of punishment. We are accustomed to take rewards for granted, but, if we ask why they make sense, the answer is that a man, by acting rightly, has shown himself to be such as to be able to appreciate and use properly any further goods or powers which are bestowed on him by way of reward. Merit and demerit correspond in the form of their ethical interpretation.

Returning to punishment, we may conclude that minor punishments, such as fines, can be construed as compensation paid to society for the enjoyment of an undue advantage. Here the punishment can be intelligibly said to negate the wrong. Greater punishments, however, such as imprisonment and death, must be understood on the ground that a wrongdoer has made himself such as no longer to be trusted to use liberty or even life rightly. Retribution, as the deprivation of these powers, can, therefore, be not only a necessary condition but a sufficient motive of punishment.

In practice, however, human judgment is fallible, and it would be rash to try to assign the appropriate measure of retribution without a further motive. Society has to protect itself against habitual criminals and to deter others from following their example. If it can bring about the reformation of the criminal by removing him from his customary surroundings, this is evidently the happiest outcome of the use of restraint and is to be pursued whenever possible. An irreversible penalty like death must be inflicted as sparingly as possible. While the retributive factor remains fundamental, an adequate appreciation of the place of punishment in practice calls neither for the exclusive consideration of retribution nor for an equally exclusive emphasis on reformation or deterrence, but for the assessment of all three factors in proportion to one another and in relation to the social purpose of law.

Chapter XI

PROPERTY

I

THE discussion of the relationship between law and morality might be taken as the opening of a treatment of social and political ethics. But political theory is rightly regarded as having sufficient scope and importance to rank as a separate study. Moreover it needs to be treated in a different way from pure ethics, for the suitability of political systems has to be judged in relation to concrete historical circumstances. There is no perfect constitution for all nations at all times. Consequently, although it is eminently desirable to discuss political problems in a philosophical manner, they are also historically conditioned problems. The solutions of the past can help us in so far as past problems resemble our own, but an attempt to discuss political theory in independence of history leads either to the enunciation of jejune copybook maxims or to the construction of impracticable utopias. There is one social problem, however, which is so fundamental and so relevant to the rightful freedom of the individual that it deserves a place here. This is the problem of property.

If I own a thing, I have the power both of using it and of excluding others from its use. But I have a power of using many things, such as air to breathe, which I do not own because all other men are equally entitled to the available air until I have actually inhaled it. When I own something I can prevent other men from using it even when I am not using it myself, and it is this power of exclusion which specifies the notion of property.

It is at once evident that the notion of property is not simple and indivisible. There is no single clearcut distinction between owning a thing and not owning it. Property rights vary in accordance with the manner and degree in which the owner or owners can exclude others from the use of the thing owned. Thus I may have a lease of certain property or a life interest in it, and these are genuine, although temporary, property rights. Otherwise I may have a right to property for certain purposes only, as I may have grazing rights or fishing rights. The question remains open whether any kind of property right can be so absolute and unconditional that the owner's power of exclusion admits of no exception.

If we are to speak clearly of the power of exclusion in which ownership consists, we must distinguish between a physical power, a legal power and a moral power. Even in the state of nature as imagined by Hobbes the strong man might be able to maintain his exclusive use of certain things; he would then have a physical power of property. Nor is this lawless physical conception of property without contemporary application in spite of all that lawyers can do; it has considerable application both in boys' schools and in international affairs. In an ordered civil society, however, the State, concentrating in itself the power of coercion, has usually recognized the property of its citizens and has lent, when required, the physical force necessary to maintain it; here we have a legal power or legal right of property. But a legal right is not necessarily coincident with a moral right, although, for the sake of the stability of society, they should no doubt be assumed to coincide unless there is positive evidence to the contrary. A moral right to property exists when the exclusive use of it can be vindicated to the owner on a genuine ethical basis.

A final discrimination must be made between ownership by a single person and ownership by a group of persons. In the latter case each person may have a definite share in the property or a definite claim to a certain proportion of it, even though the parts be not allotted. Such a condition, although it may in a certain sense be described as common ownership, is evidently reducible to the notion of private property. There is common ownership in a full sense when each can take what he wants from the common store. Thus, in a family, although the householder may be the legal owner, the members of the family really use house and furniture for most purposes in common, and it will be recognized that, as members of the family, they have a right to do so. What is usually described as communism, the common ownership of the means of production, distribution and exchange, differs both from the complex form of private property of which a limited liability company is an instance, and from the element of natural communism which appears in a normal household. As we all know, it really means ownership by the State. It might be ownership on behalf of the people, but it would not be ownership by the people, except in the limited sense in which they could by their voting powers produce an effect on the administration of such property. For only officials, not individual citizens at their will, would immediately exert property rights over it. Our individual rights at a railway station have not changed in any respect since the lines were converted into British Railways.

Such is a summary analysis of the notion of property. This involves a discrimination between the power to use a thing and the power to exclude others from the use of it; between physical, moral and legal power; and between private ownership, common ownership and ownership by the State.

II

In discussing the ethical basis of property there are a few points which it is fortunately possible to assume as obvious. It is obvious that mankind in general, as needing material things and having the capacity to adapt them to its needs, has a certain right of dominion over them. It is equally obvious that there is no immediate natural designation of particular men to own particular things. It is obvious, too, that in actual consumption there must be private appropriation, since two men cannot simultaneously wear the same shirt or eat the same piece of bread. The need for discussion appears when we ask whether the ownership of goods in store and of capital goods should be private or common.

The first developed defence of private property is Aristotle's answer to the communism of Plato's *Republic*. Plato's communism should not, of course, be exaggerated, for he suggests only that there should be common ownership among the guardians of the State in order to lead them to a life of disinterested service. Such common ownership among a minority of specially selected persons resembles modern political communism less than the communism of a religious order. In any case it has no place in the *Laws*, where Plato is concerned rather with practical legislation to prevent the richer citizens from acquiring too much and to help the poorer to obtain enough.

When Aristotle criticizes the *Republic*, he remarks in effect that communistic proposals sound very well when they suggest that everyone is going to live in peace and harmony with the ugliest cause of human disputes removed. But is it really true that disputes about material goods are due to the existence of private property? Are they not mainly due to a lack of clear and equitable demarcation of property rights? This being so, if all things were held in common and everyone were dependent on others for his share, there would be not less but more jealousy and controversy. It would be like a group of travellers, who tend to quarrel because they are too much thrown together in small matters.

Aristotle adds another reason in favour of private property when he says that men naturally pay more attention to their own business than they do to that of others. Hence the institution of private property promotes general prosperity. A more fundamental ground lies in the rightful demands of human personality, for the satisfaction which a man finds in ownership is a sign of a natural tendency to extend his personality into the domain of material things. Therein he develops himself and obtains a wider field for the exercise of ethical activity.[1]

Aquinas follows Aristotle closely in his defence of private property, maintaining that it conduces to peace when everyone has his own and that men will look after their own affairs more carefully than those of the community. A communistic state, he remarks, would be like a household with a great number of servants, where every job is left to someone else. This he may have had early opportunity of observing in his father's feudal castle, and it may not be without some relevance to contemporary bureaucratic methods.[2]

These are good reasons in favour of private property, but we cannot say that they settle the whole question. In the first place, they are reasons of expediency, based upon the observed results of private as compared with common ownership. Such reasons are liable to be countered by other reasons of general or particular expediency.

Secondly, although they are good grounds for the institution of private property in general, they do not tell us what is the foundation of the right of *this* man to own *this* piece of property. The medieval jurists, however, did not neglect this question, and they usually answered it by a generalization of the Roman legal theory of *occupatio*, the taking into possession of that which has no owner. "Quod nullius est", say the *Institutes* of Justinian, "id naturali ratione occupanti conceditur."[3] In a settled state of society things without owners are rare, and the maxim that finding is keeping has a comparatively limited application. In a primitive condition, however, in which things had not yet been divided, the medieval jurists were able to find an open field for the doctrine of *occupatio*.

A man, having not only present but also future needs, which he can foresee and for which he must provide, is entitled to

---

[1] Aristotle, *Politics*, II ii, 1262 b – 1263 b.
[2] Aquinas, *Summa*, II^a, II^{ae}, qu. 66, art. ii.
[3] Justinian, *Institutes*, lib. ii, tit. i.

assume the ownership of what he requires, so long as no one else has already done so. The original title to property must, therefore, be found in a primitive occupation or taking into possession of things hitherto unoccupied. But it is evident that this theory is still incomplete. If a mere assertion of ownership were enough, this would amount to what has been called the divine right of grab. The things of which possession is taken must be things which a man really needs and upon which he exercises his activity. The act of occupation itself demands labour, as when food is gathered to be stored for future use, and possession is usually exercised in recurrent labour, as when land is taken to be tilled. Hence the occupation theory of property needs to be completed by a labour theory. This combination of ideas is most familiar to us in Locke's discussion of the question.

Labour, says Locke, is unquestionably the property of the man who labours. "Whatsoever, then, he removes out of the state that Nature hath provided and left it in, he hath mixed his labour with it, and joined to it something which is his own, and thereby makes it his property."[1] Before the earth and its products were appropriated, then, they could be taken into possession by anyone who mixed his labour with them. This appropriation was just, provided that no one took more than he could use, since there was as much and as good left over for others to take. From this original title all other titles, by inheritance or exchange, are derived.

We could wish that Locke had been explicit about the position of the man who has nothing but his labour when the land and its products have already been appropriated. Nor is the logical transition from property in labour to property in that with which labour is mixed altogether pellucid. Locke, indeed, is a pioneer in another well-trodden direction when he tries to show that all, or nearly all, economic value is the result of labour. He compares the negligible value of waste land with the value of cultivated land, forgetting that, where land is short, the value

[1] Locke, *Second Treatise of Civil Government*, ch. v.

of land which is not yet cultivated but is capable of cultivation is by no means negligible.

With these weaknesses in Locke's theory it is not surprising that similar premises should with other thinkers have led to precisely opposite conclusions. For, while Locke is the classical defender of the pure individualistic view of property, the fundamental socialistic argument is equally based on the exclusive value of labour. The modern capitalistic system is indicted because in it money has usurped the place naturally belonging to labour as the source of value. It is money which becomes fruitful, while labour is treated as a commodity to be bought as cheaply as possible, that is, at the bare cost of its maintenance and reproduction. Consequently, beyond what the labourer receives for his toil, he produces a surplus value which goes into the pocket of the capitalist. While, with the development of industry on a large scale, the mode of production has become social, its profits are appropriated by a few fortunate individuals who are the possessors of capital.

Thus there is a contradiction between labour producing value and capital absorbing it, between social production and individual appropriation. The contradiction can be resolved only by the workers seizing control of capital and so recapturing the fruits of their labour. Under modern industrial conditions this implies social ownership of the means of production, distribution and exchange.

Locke, on the ground that labour is the title to property, justifies the appropriation of natural wealth by the first comers who enjoy the opportunity of mixing their labour with it. The socialists, on the same ground that labour is the title to property, contend that no individual should appropriate natural wealth and that the whole fruits of industry should go to those who are actually engaged in working in it. This would be an extremely piquant theoretical contradiction if it were not also a source of practical unrest.

III

What has happened is that each side has inflated relevant partial considerations into absolute and exclusive rights. It must be noticed in the first place that man is not a creator but an artificer; he does not bring things into being out of nothingness but modifies already existent things in order to serve his needs. Hence everything which a man may possess has at bottom its natural being which he did not make and which was not of itself destined for his exclusive use. No property right is so absolute that it can never be justifiably modified or superseded for the sake of those whose need is more urgent.

Both effective occupation by labour in the past and the application of present labour are sources of moral claims, neither of which destroys the other. The satisfaction of these claims in due proportion is not to be left simply to the operation of economic forces, for this is a question of the rights of persons. The business of a social and legal system, here as in other matters, is to make an equitable transformation of these necessarily vague moral claims into clearly defined rights of this man to this and of that man to that. It is not in the power of man to secure ideal justice, but, if there is no perfect social system, there are many tolerable ones. While every effort is worth making to arrive at a fair system of property rights in accordance with the circumstances of the time, no specific order of property seems by itself to be worth giving one's life to establish or to uphold.

It is unfortunate, however, if we are left with a choice between effective ownership by a few and ownership by the State or by bodies set up by the State. For the State should, as far as possible, stand as an impartial organ of justice above the field of economic rivalry. If it becomes a competitor in this field, it can far too easily seize unfair advantages for itself, and, if it becomes the sole big employer, its capacity for tyranny is almost unlimited.

Moreover, the general arguments of expediency in favour of a wide diffusion of property rights remain, and there do not seem to be any equally weighty arguments to the contrary. A wide diffusion of property is the best guarantee both of individual freedom and of contentment in work. A man needs to feel some control over his work in order to make it an interest in life and not merely a means of subsistence. Hence a sound social policy, correcting excessive inequality without suppressing the greater rewards due to superior skill and effort, should aim at providing as many men as possible with a personal stake in their work and with security in the possession of what they require for themselves and their families.

Chapter XII

BEYOND MORALITY

I

A SURVEY of the field of morality shows us with duties which arise from our own natures and duties which have their source in our relations with our fellows. There is also the invitation to go beyond strict duty towards a fuller moral development. This can be summed up in self-realization in the narrower sense and what Bradley called "my station and its duties". But Bradley was convinced that all this is evidently incomplete and points forward to "ideal morality".

The incompleteness of mere morality has been felt in different ways by different thinkers. If the final purpose of right action is said to be self-fulfilment, as it was by Aristotle, we are at once led to protest that altruism has an essential, and perhaps the chief, place in a moral outlook. Self-sacrifice is not to be forgotten, nor should it be explained away, as it would be if it were justified in the last resort as a contribution to self-realization. It is a moral value which is all the higher the more it is a genuine abdication of the claims of the self for the sake of a greater good.

Yet our human moral efforts might seem rather futile if they were not endorsed in the end by the course of the universe. It is noteworthy that a philosopher who insisted as much on duty for duty's sake as Kant did thought that the validity of the moral imperative postulated a moral ordering of the universe. The moral law would not stand unless there were a God who provided in the end that virtue was requited with happiness.

We may well think that Kant exaggerated here and that we

could be content with that kind of happiness which is the satisfaction of having acted rightly, without looking for any further reward or any perfect proportion between virtue and happiness in a wider sense. If we could not thus be content, the proper disinterestedness of morality would disappear.

Even so the incompleteness of mere morality can be felt in another way. For moral relations to others are of their nature external. Justice consists in giving their due to others precisely as others and in so far as these others have claims upon us. Strict justice is admirable but not warming, and even beneficence which exceeds strict justice is less than it might be if it is only the fullness of morality. In other words, we expect instinctively that morality should be completed by something in the nature of love or friendship. But that calls for deeper reflection.

II

Aristotle was sufficiently convinced of the importance for the good life of associations between man and man to devote to their discussion two books, the eighth and the ninth, of the *Ethics*. From true friendship he discriminated those associations for the sake of mutual benefit which sometimes masquerade as friendships. If men cultivate one another for the sake of what they can do for one another, even if their mutual benefits are of the worthiest kind, this is plainly not what we really mean by friendship. Nor can true friendship be identified with those associations for the sake of pleasure which also are often mistaken for it. In modern terms, the people with whom we play golf or bridge may seem inseparable from us, but they are inseparable only as long as they are found necessary or useful in our recreations. If they ceased to be able to play, we should drop them without compunction. By contrast, true friendship depends on genuine sympathy, a real community of interest in things thought to be worth while for their own sake.

In his book, *Pour l'histoire du problème de l'amour au Moyen Age*, Pierre Rousselot spoke of two opposed theories of love among the medieval thinkers. For the so-called physical theory of love, what was involved was an extension to another of an attitude which you naturally had towards yourself; for the ecstatic theory love involved a forgetfulness of self, a losing of yourself in others. These theories are not as opposed as they seem, for they are both inadequate ways of saying the same thing. The point about love is that the barriers are down and that the distinction between self and other becomes irrelevant to feeling and action. It matters little whether you describe this sort of unity as the self absorbing the other or as the other absorbing the self; what matters is the resultant unity for feeling and action.

Where there is love, therefore, or friendship in the full sense of the word, the contrast between egoism and altruism, selfishness and self-sacrifice, ceases to affect the situation. The friend is as happy in the happiness of his friend as he is in his own. No difficulty could, then, be felt any longer about the literalness or ultimacy of the moral demand for self-sacrifice, for it would cease to be merely a moral demand on behalf of another and would become a joy in the advantage of the other.

This description, however, true as it is of love or friendship in the full sense, calls forth a less inspiring reflection. For it shows us how rare such a complete unity of persons is. Very few instances of love or friendship, even though they deserve the name in their degree, reach the fullness which is their ideal form. The story of human affections, although they contain so much of what is finest in man, is full also of disillusionment and failure.

If, then, morality is to achieve its proper transcendence, not only partially and in a few cases but with some approach to universality, it can only be in some way by which the attitude of love can be directed towards the universe as a whole. And this can only be through our acknowledgment of the divine in it or of the divine which is its source. The proper transcendence of mere morality lies in the love of God. Morality does not by itself provide us with a religion, but it points towards a religious attitude to the world as the only final dissipation of its obscurities and completion of its inadequacies. The study of morality as such, however, retains its value both because it yields truth on its own level and because without it we could not understand what is needed in order to go beyond it.